D1272026

ST ANTONY'S PAPERS · NUMBER 9

★

INTERNATIONAL
COMMUNISM

ST ANTONY'S PAPERS

★

ST ANTONY'S PAPERS · NUMBER 9

INTERNATIONAL COMMUNISM

EDITED BY

DAVID FOOTMAN

1960
Southern Illinois University Press
Carbondale, Illinois

PUBLISHED IN
GREAT BRITAIN, 1960, BY
CHATTO AND WINDUS LTD

★

PUBLISHED IN
THE UNITED STATES, 1960, BY
SOUTHERN ILLINOIS
UNIVERSITY PRESS

★

LIBRARY OF CONGRESS CATALOG
CARD NUMBER 60-13451

HX
40
F68

PRINTED IN GREAT BRITAIN BY
BUTLER AND TANNER LTD
FROME AND LONDON

Sept. '66

CONTENTS

This volume is intended by the Warden and Fellows of St Antony's College to serve as a tribute to the memory of their friend and colleague, Robert Nigel Carew Hunt. His paper on Muenzenberg was completed shortly before his death; the other contributors were all associated with him in his Seminar on International Communism.

The main emphasis of the work of St Antony's College, Oxford, since its foundation in 1950 has been in the fields of modern history and international affairs. The College organizes a number of regular Seminars at which are read papers produced by its members in the course of their research or by visiting experts from other institutions. The College further sponsors the delivery of lectures in Oxford by scholars of international reputation in their respective fields.

An appreciable volume of contribution to scholarship is thus being produced under the auspices of St Antony's, and the present series has been started in order to preserve and present a selection of this work. This series is not, however, confined to this material alone and includes contributions from other places.

Three numbers a year are issued and each number is devoted to a particular topic or a particular part of the world.

UNITED FRONT TACTICS IN THE
COMINTERN 1921–1928

By Jane Degras

UNITED FRONT TACTICS, adopted by the Communist International at the end of 1921, and pursued until the spring of 1928, were an implicit admission that the International had been founded on a misconception. The bolshevik leaders had believed that the revolution in Russia was only a beginning and would soon spread to other countries. The working class, they thought, were revolutionary in temper and intention; what was holding them back was the policy of their leaders, who had betrayed them in 1914 and were prepared to do so again. It was therefore necessary to detach the labour rank and file from their leaders, and provide a consciously revolutionary leadership for the supposedly revolutionary masses. This, essentially, was the origin of the Communist International; rather more than a year later, when the initial advances of the Red Army in the war with Poland encouraged hopes that the revolution was about to spread, a new trade union international was established (RILU).

These hopes, undermined by the failure of the Red Army to win local support in Poland and by its subsequent retreat, were abandoned, more or less officially, in the spring of 1921 with the collapse of the so-called March action in Germany—an ill-considered attempt at insurrection which Paul Levi, shortly afterwards expelled from the German Communist Party, condemned as a *putsch*. In Germany, as in the country to which they looked as their model, the communists were isolated. If it was to exert influence on the labour movement, the Comintern had to re-establish the links broken in 1919, just as Russia, if it was to survive, had to conciliate its opponents at home, to reach agreement with its neighbours, and resume normal business intercourse with the outside world. As on many other occasions, the change in Comintern policy was both stimulated by and in its turn reinforced a parallel change in Soviet domestic policy, this time the retreat into

9

the new economic policy ordered after the suppression of the Kronstadt rising. At the ECCI meeting in February 1922 Zinoviev said:

"Had the Red Army in 1920 taken Warsaw, the tactics of the CI today would be other than they are . . . the strategic setback was followed by a political setback for the whole workers' movement —the Russian proletarian party was compelled to make extensive concessions . . . that slowed down the tempo of the proletarian revolution; but the reverse is also true; the setback which the proletariat of the western European countries suffered from 1919 to 1921 influenced the policy of the first proletarian state and slowed down the tempo in Russia."

More than two years later, at the fifth Comintern congress, he said that the RILU had been

"founded at a moment when it seemed that we would be able to break through the enemy's front by a frontal attack and quickly capture the unions . . . all the tactical difficulties of the CI in these five years have arisen precisely because the development was much slower than was thought . . . Now we must fight social-democracy by roundabout means."

With the third Comintern congress (June–July 1921), Trotsky wrote later, "it is realized that the post-war revolutionary ferment is over". Lenin, using Japanese action at Port Arthur as an analogy, said that the Comintern had passed from the tactics of assault to the tactics of siege. The "theses on tactics" adopted by the congress, acknowledging that "the majority of the workers are not yet under communist influence", made it the primary task of the communist parties to win their adherence. "The watchwords and principles of the communist parties provide the only ground on which the working masses can again unite." Always sensitive to the charge of having split the labour movement, the Comintern sought to shift the burden on to other shoulders. Since its programme expressed "the necessities of the proletarian struggle . . . it is now the social-democratic and centrist parties and groups which reflect the dispersal and division of the forces of the proletariat, while the communist parties represent the element of concentration". More than four years later the same argument was advanced in the theses for propagandists issued on the second anniversary of Lenin's death: the working class had in fact been split—horizontally— by the attitude of the socialists on the outbreak of war in 1914. The

Comintern saved the cause by changing the horizontal into a vertical split which separated the workers, not by country, but into revolutionaries and reformists. Unity on an opportunist basis was destroyed in order that proletarian unity might be erected "on a higher basis". This was the only possible method of establishing unity "so long as the revolutionary wave was advancing". Now that it had ebbed, other methods had to be found.

The new tactics were elaborated in the "Directives on the united front" adopted by the Comintern Executive (ECCI) on 18 December 1921. The united front was defined briefly as a method of organizing the masses on a programme of transitional demands. Introducing them, Zinoviev said that the workers attributed their defeats since the war to their disunity, and a united front policy would win their allegiance. He denied any incompatibility between this policy and the attempt to attract unions from the IFTU into the RILU; united front action could not be taken except on communist terms. To the question, why split if you want a united front, he replied:

"This is a dialectical question which every communist must understand. Precisely because it is an epoch of splits, and because we have now become a force, we can on certain conditions work together with the Second and Two-and-a-half Internationals . . . But if we had not made the split, we would not be the factor which we now are, and could not carry this manœuvre through. It is possible we shall have to carry out many more splits, and we shall still go to the socialists and say: 'Yes, we want unity; unity on this platform'."

In an article published on the last day of the year Radek wrote that the object of communist work inside the social-democratic parties was to win them or split them. A year later, at the fourth Comintern congress which endorsed the new line, Radek returned to this theme. "We entered on this road not because we want to merge with the social democrats, but in the knowledge that we shall stifle them in our embrace."

The theses stated that,

"Having secured organizational freedom to influence the working masses by their propaganda, the communist parties of all countries are now trying to achieve the broadest and most complete unity possible on practical action. The Amsterdamers and the heroes of the Second International preach this unity in words, but in their actions work against it . . . They are now seeking a way out of the deadlock for which they are themselves responsible by initiating splits, by disorganizing and sabotaging the struggle of the working masses."

If it reached agreement with any party belonging to the other two Internationals, a communist party was to retain "complete freedom to put forward its own views and to criticize the opponents of communism . . . Whenever the offer of a joint struggle is rejected by our opponents the masses must be informed of this and thus learn who are the real destroyers of the workers' united front."

The Executive met a great deal of opposition to the new policy, particularly from the French, Italian, and Spanish representatives. They argued that since the chief burden of their propaganda had been that the social-democrats were the worst enemies of the working class, the new tactics would puzzle and confuse their own parties and the workers they were trying to win. How could they ask their members to work with parties which for the last three years they had been accusing of treachery, and doing their best to split and to wreck? The attitude of the French and Italian delegates was endorsed by their parties; as a matter of communist discipline the theses were passed, but at the request of the French CP the question was put on the agenda of the fourth CI congress which met at the end of 1922. There the "tactical theses", elaborating those adopted a year earlier, were passed unanimously, although Bukharin informed the Russian party that of the replies to an ECCI questionnaire sent out shortly before the congress, 69 per cent of the French opposed united front tactics, 40 per cent of the German, 26 per cent of the Italian, and 24 per cent of the British. The theses, however, noted that in France "the course of events has convinced even those who a short time ago were on principle hostile to this tactic of the necessity of its employment".

Those who persisted in their opposition to the united front policy were rebuked as sectarians. This became the preferred term of abuse applied to those who, when united front tactics were in official favour, advocated a strictly revolutionary class policy. Conversely, when united front tactics fell out of favour, those who advocated them were rebuked as opportunists, willing to sacrifice principle for the sake of an illusory temporary advantage.

It was in fact the adoption of the united front policy which introduced into the Comintern the concept of deviation. Collaboration with the social democrats, implied in the policy, was a denial of all the principles which the Comintern had been founded to promote. It was a policy of pure expediency, in which right and left were no longer actual positions, but errors in timing. For a revolutionary party, the united front was inherently contradictory. Since it eliminated any stable principle against which action and policy could be measured, the only criterion was the decision handed down by the authorities, and an authoritarian concept of party discipline and unity was the inescapable corollary. Comintern and communist party policies could no longer be judged as orthodox or not by the criterion of content, or by their compatibility with the doctrinal canon, but only by the degree to which they conformed with or deviated from Comintern decisions as interpreted at any given time.

Constantly under attack, the new line was as constantly in need of definition. At the meeting of the ECCI in June 1923 Zinoviev referred to it as a strategic manœuvre. "It consists in our appealing constantly to people who, we know in advance, will not go along with us." Asked by Treint whether united front tactics were compatible with the insulting language they used about social democracy and whether they should openly admit the nature of this "strategic manœuvre", he said: "I am unconditionally in favour of any stratagem in the fight against an irreconcilable enemy, but only if it does not demoralize our own army."

A joint manifesto published by the ECCI and the RILU executive urged workers to force their leaders into a united front. "And if they stand out stubbornly against it, bring about a united front over their heads." In the same manifesto, the charge of splitting was transferred to the reformists who, in their anxiety "to rebuild the capitalist world at the expense of the working class . . . have to split the trade unions and the labour movement". The charge was repeated in an ECCI letter to a conference called by the German CP to discuss the occupation of the Ruhr. "The working classes are helpless and split because the Second and the Amsterdam Internationals split them and so made them helpless. If the leaders were ready to form and operate a united front with the communists, the working class would have stronger forces."

The first major attempt to operate the new line was made when the Vienna Union of socialist parties—the Two-and-a-half International —in agreement with the Second International, called a conference of representatives of the three Internationals (and of the Italian Socialist Party, which was affiliated to none of them) in Berlin in April 1922.

The ECCI accepted the invitation, against the opposition of the representatives of the French, Italian, and Spanish communist parties. The conference was the scene of bitter recriminations between the delegates of the Second and Third Internationals: the agreement to set up a committee of nine to continue its work was pointless; at its first and only meeting on 23 May, which failed to reach agreement, the ECCI delegation withdrew. At the ECCI meeting in June Zinoviev said that the attempt had nevertheless been useful, because the communists could now no longer be accused of being the splitters. (Radek thought it was not only the socialist leaders who were to blame—the masses wanted unity, but were reluctant to fight for it.) The conclusions drawn from the failure of this attempt were reflected in the statement issued by the ECCI at the end of April:

> "The united front is not and should not be merely a fraternisation of party leaders . . . The united front means the association of all workers . . . against the bourgeoisie, with the leaders if they want it so, without the leaders if they remain indifferently aside, and in defiance of the leaders and against the leaders if they sabotage the workers' united front."

The statement issued after the breakdown of the committee ended with the words: "Fight the leaders of the Second International who are splitting the working class. Build the united front from below." The same dialectical note, too subtle for most of the communists trying to operate the policy, was sounded a year later, when the Second and Vienna Internationals amalgamated: "The communists split the social-democratic parties led by traitors in order to unite the proletariat; the reformists will unite in Hamburg in order to split the proletariat again."

After the fiasco of the KPD attempt at insurrection in October 1923 the policy had to be modified to exclude "combinations from above". For a few days the communists in the Saxon and Thuringian diets had formed coalition governments with the social-democrats, and the collapse of the projected insurrection was officially attributed by the Comintern to the "treachery" of the SPD. The ECCI Presidium statement of 19 January 1924 urged parties to understand that the united front did not mean "a democratic coalition, an alliance with social-democracy . . . United front tactics have a meaning for the CI only if they promote the object of winning the bulk of the proletariat for the revolutionary struggle for power." They were intended to accelerate the collapse of the social-democratic parties. Henceforth there could only be united front tactics from below. In Germany the goal was the political annihilation of the SPD.

Disappointing as the results had been, the tactics were to be continued. (To have rejected them would have been a tacit admission that there was no revolutionary situation in Germany.) The circular on the agenda of the fifth Comintern congress stated that they "remain correct for an entire epoch. It is merely necessary to take stronger precautionary measures against their distortion." The resolution of the congress on the report of the ECCI "vigorously rejected all opportunist interpretations of united front tactics, as well as every attempt to build them up into anything more than a revolutionary method of agitation and of mobilizing the masses".

The tactical theses adopted by the congress explained that

"while for the CI the main purpose of united front tactics consists in the struggle *against* the leaders of counter-revolutionary social-democracy and in emancipating social-democratic workers from their influence, the representatives of the right-wing tendency [in the Comintern] tend to interpret the united front as a political alliance *with* social-democracy."

The theses laid down that united front tactics from below were always necessary (except possibly at a decisive moment in the class war), that these could be combined with negotiations with social-democratic leaders, but that in no circumstances could the united front "only from above" be permitted. The united front must always be under CP leadership. It was designed to detach the workers from their treacherous counter-revolutionary leaders. At the fifth ECCI plenum (March–April 1925) Kuusinen repeated the warning; though the social-democratic leaders might for a time be prepared to act with the communists, "we must always fight them, expose them, and defeat them".

In under-developed countries, where there was no labour movement of any size or significance to which overtures for a united front could be made, attention was turned to the nationalist organizations representing the "struggle for liberation from colonial oppression". The outstanding example was China, where the united front took the form of collaboration with the Kuomintang. Soviet policy towards the KMT was, of course, more broadly based than this phrase would suggest. It is only necessary to read Lenin's theses on the colonial question, adopted by the second Comintern congress in 1920, to grasp the significance of the part assigned to anti-imperialist movements in the general context of Soviet and communist strategy. Nevertheless, characteristic features of that strategy at any particular time were largely shaped by tactical ideas which to the Comintern appeared to have universal validity.

The first congress of the Chinese CP in July 1921 decided, at the suggestion of the Comintern representative Sneevliet (Maring), and against considerable opposition, to form an alliance with the KMT; their manifesto of June 1922 described it as a "united front of democratic revolution". This became known as the "bloc without" and was succeeded, in August 1922, by the "bloc within", which meant that members of the CP became individual members of the KMT. This decision, again, was taken under pressure from Maring, and against even stronger opposition.

In this respect the united front in China differed radically from its counterpart in the industrialized countries; there the communists had been warned that they were on no account to lose or submerge their identity in the wider movement, to accept any discipline but their own, subscribe to any principles but those formulated by the Comintern. In China, on the ground that the KMT was not primarily a class party, but a party of all anti-imperialist groups and classes, and that neither socialism nor a Soviet republic could possibly be established in China in the near future, the strict preservation of the communists' identity was said to be unnecessary. This was, apparently, a *post hoc* rationalization of a concession forced on Moscow by Sun Yat-sen, the Kuomintang leader, who would accept alliance with the communists on no other terms than their submission to KMT discipline. It was, of course, admitted in the Comintern that the national bourgeoisie could not be a permanent ally, for it was to be expected that with the development of the class struggle their fear of proletarian and peasant movements would push them into a more conciliatory attitude towards imperialism, if not an outright alliance, to fight the social revolution; until this happened, however, the united front policy gave the communists access to the masses, and the opportunity to influence the growing nationalist movement.

The dispute ended only with the complete breakdown of the CCP–KMT alliance in 1927. In the intervening years, within the Comintern as well as its Chinese section, KMT–CCP relations were the subject of endless analysis and disagreement. Rarely indeed was the case argued on its merits, for towards the end it became one of the questions most bitterly in dispute within the politbureau of the CPSU. In consequence, the policy was pursued far beyond the point where it continued to pay dividends. By the spring of 1926 the communist position in the KMT became precarious; Chiang-Kai-shek felt strong enough, if not to dispense with communist aid, then at least to exact a price for refraining from turning against them; on 20 March he arrested the political commissars (largely communist) in the army and placed his Soviet advisers under house arrest. A number of the leading Chinese communists urged that the party should revert to the policy of the "bloc without", but the policy-makers in Moscow, counting on China as an ally against possible hostile Anglo-Japanese action, were determined to preserve good relations with Chiang. Upon the Russians' undertaking to support the KMT army's northern expedition —the final goal of which was the capture of Peking—Chiang released his prisoners, reinstated most of his advisers, and reaffirmed his loyalty to the Comintern.

But the united front dilemma remained and indeed became more pointed. Since in theory the communist party had to stand and act as an independent class party, the policy of watering down its programme to suit the immediate needs of the bourgeoisie provided the CPSU opposition with an excellent debating point. Stalin and his supporters argued that since the struggle in China at that stage was primarily an anti-imperialist struggle, it was correct to restrain the Chinese workers and peasants from hostile action against the landlords and capitalists who supported the national revolution.

"The point", he said, "lies not only in the bourgeois-democratic character of the Canton government, which is the embryo of the future all-China revolutionary government; the point is above all that this government is, and cannot but be, an anti-imperialist government, that every advance it makes is a blow at world imperialism . . . It is said that the Chinese communists should withdraw from the Kuomintang. That would be wrong comrades . . . The whole course, character, and prospects of the Chinese revolution undoubtedly testify in favour of the Chinese communists remaining in the Kuomintang and intensifying their work in it."

Trotsky and his supporters, on the other hand, considered it

"a gross mistake to think that imperialism mechanically welds together all the classes of China from without . . . The revolutionary struggle against imperialism does not weaken, but rather strengthens the political differentiation of the classes . . . The struggle against imperialism, precisely because of its economic and military power, demands a powerful exertion of forces from the very depths of the Chinese people. Really to arouse the workers and peasants against imperialism is possible only by connecting their basic and most profound life interests with the cause of the country's liberation . . . But everything that brings the oppressed and exploited masses of the toilers to their feet inevitably pushes the national bourgeoisie into an open bloc with the imperialists. The class struggle between the bourgeoisie and the masses of workers and peasants is not weakened but, on the contrary, it is sharpened by imperialist oppression."

The course of the dispute has been charted in many studies (most recently and brilliantly by Conrad Brandt) and need not be recapitulated here. The decision was taken out of the Comintern's hands by Chiang Kai-shek, who in April 1927, having reached Shanghai in the first stage of the northern expedition, turned openly and unequivocally on his communist allies and did his best to exterminate them. Responsibility for continuing the united front policy too long was then placed unblushingly on the shoulders of the Chinese central committee, more particularly on those who had consistently opposed it.

The other outstanding example of united front policy, and its failure, was the Anglo-Russian trade union unity committee. This had been started with high hopes in 1924 and endorsed by the TUC and the Russian trade union central council in the following year. The fifth plenum of the ECCI, meeting in April 1925, passed a resolution on trade union unity which contained the following passage:

> "The enlarged session of the ECCI attaches immense importance to the rapprochement between the English and Soviet trade unions, in which it sees a pledge that the international unity of the trade union movement is beginning to take practical shape. The enlarged Executive welcomes the activities of the Anglo-Russian trade union conference and calls on workers of all countries, without distinction of political belief, to support resolutely and energetically the formation of the Anglo-Soviet trade union bloc."

In speaking to the resolution, Lozovsky regretted that some Comintern sections regarded the committee as "just a manœuvre". This opinion was apparently shared by the majority in the IFTU Council which, in February 1925, rejected the British proposal for a conference between the IFTU and the Russian unions; the Russian unions, it was said, wanted not to join but to capture the IFTU. At the end of the year Zinoviev, at the CPSU congress, described the committee as a brilliant demonstration of the correctness of united front tactics.

The value of the committee was put to the proof at the time of the General Strike. Before the strike had begun, the ECCI and RILU issued appeals and manifestoes on its significance, warning "the working masses, who are ready for the fight", that their leaders were irresolute and some were prepared to betray them. Even "the left-wing leaders of the Labour Party and the unions are showing themselves unequal to the situation". Only the CPGB and the Minority Movement "advocated the militant unity of the trade union movement in Great Britain and throughout the world".

On the collapse of the strike, the British communist leaders were reprimanded for their failure to criticize the TUC openly and sharply enough. The Russian trade union central council published a bitter attack on the General Council for its "treachery" which several members of the British central committee considered too hostile. At the ECCI presidium meeting in August Murphy explained that an attack on their leaders was regarded by the British workers as an attack on their unions. (He was later won over to the Russian view.) At the meeting of the joint committee, convened at the request of the Russian side and held in Paris at the end of July, the British side asked that the charge of "treachery" should be withdrawn; the Russian representatives refused, and the meeting was adjourned. (It reconvened in Berlin in August, but with no greater success.)

The policy of maintaining the committee in existence, like the policy of collaboration with the KMT, became a prime target of the opposition in the CPSU and the Comintern. When the TUC General Council rejected the offer of a large sum of money from the Russian unions Trotsky wrote that this was bound to surprise the Russian people who had so far not seen in the Russian press any criticism of the General Council; the Soviet side of the committee had surrendered the right of criticism which was an essential corollary of united front policy, and the CPGB had followed their example. Once the General Council had betrayed the strike, he wrote later, the committee merely helped them to conceal their treachery from the masses. Capitalist stabilization in England rested on Labour Party and TUC support of the bourgeoisie, and it was disgraceful to act in concert with them.

Stalin justified the policy of remaining on the committee on two grounds. At the meeting of the CC of the CPSU on 15 July 1926 he said that the committee enabled the Russian unions to strengthen their connexions with the trade union movement in the West, and to revolutionize it; it also served the struggle against imperialist war, and in particular the struggle against imperialist intervention in the Soviet Union. One of its tasks was to "widen the fissure between Amsterdam (i.e., the IFTU) and the British trade union movement", and to create conditions promoting communist leadership of the unions. He repeated these arguments at the ECCI presidium on 7 August, where he attacked Murphy for saying that the CPGB resented interference from the Russian unions. The General Council had committed a "whole chain of betrayals". How this was to be reconciled with his statement in the same speech that the purpose of the bloc (i.e., a bloc with traitors) was "joint action in the interests of the working class" was not made clear; it was a contradiction on which Trotsky seized with relish. The argument that the committee was a bond with the masses, he wrote later, was equivalent to saying that strikebreakers served as a bond with the strikers; nor did it strengthen the Soviet position internationally—the agents of imperialism could never protect the revolution from imperialism. In a paper dated 19 September 1926 he wrote that the Comintern was substituting diplomacy for policy; all the arguments in favour of maintaining the committee applied with even greater force to entering the IFTU. Vuyovich, at the ECCI meeting at the end of the year, argued that the existence of the committee hampered those trade unionists who were trying to get rid of the reformist leaders; how could they oppose them when the Russian unions collaborated with them? After the exchange of notes between the British and Soviet governments (which led eventually to the severance of relations) early in 1927, Trotsky commented on the silence of the committee. "If it exists, why is it silent? And if it does not exist, why is there silence about its death?"

The committee did in fact meet again, in Berlin in March 1927, and agreed on a formula approving non-intervention in each other's affairs, which Trotsky called treachery to the Minority Movement. There was as much reason to break with Citrine as there had been with Chiang Kai-shek. At a further meeting of the committee, convened at Russian request in June to discuss "the war danger", no agreement was reached, and the correspondence between the two sides of the committee was then published, without prior consultation with the British, in the Russian press. The British press reproduced the Russian charges on

28 July, with the comment that it was difficult to understand the Russian trade union leaders' desire to continue to co-operate with traitors, saboteurs, and lackeys.

Again the decision was taken out of the Russians' hands; at the Edinburgh trade union congress in the autumn the General Council withdrew from the committee. The Soviet side accused the TUC of "desertion" at the very moment when the committee was most needed—after the rupture of Anglo-Soviet diplomatic relations. This, said Trotsky, was in itself a condemnation of the policy that had been pursued. Was it not natural that "traitors" should "desert"?

The failure of these two experiments in united front tactics made a change inevitable, and this could be done the more easily since by that time the opposition in the CPSU had been defeated, and its supporters in other Comintern sections—who had accused the Russians of putting their state interests above those of the revolutionary movement—had been expelled or were about to be.

The theoretical justification for the change was formulated in the resolutions of the ninth plenum of the ECCI in February 1928, and outlined before it opened in an article in *Pravda* which argued that the movement of the masses to the left, and of their reformist leaders to the right, made it necessary to fight international social-democracy even more vigorously than before. The plenum resolution on the situation in Britain stated that the Labour Party was rapidly losing the character and influence which had made Lenin insist, eight years previously, on the communists working inside it. It was now rapidly becoming an ordinary social-democratic party. As one of the speakers said, the CPGB could win leadership of the workers "only over its dead body". The majority of the British delegates did not share this view—the CPGB congress in the previous October had reaffirmed the old policy—but were persuaded to approve the resolution, which was endorsed, on their return to England, by their central committee. It implied, *inter alia,* communist candidates standing in opposition to Labour Party candidates at elections. Later in the year, at the sixth Comintern congress, Bukharin singled out Britain to illustrate the turn to the left made in the past year. "As to the English party, we have broken with all the old traditions of the English labour movement." The strongest tradition was that of a united organized working class; this was the reformists' trump card and the greatest obstacle to the liberation of the proletariat from reformist influence, for it was used to fight revolutionary ideas and the revolutionary party.

The plenum adopted a parallel resolution on France, where it had been customary for the strongest left-wing candidate in the first electoral round to receive the support of other left-wing candidates in the second round in order to defeat right-wing candidates. The new line made no distinction between the extreme right in French politics and the left-wing socialists—but an exception was made where considerations of Soviet foreign policy might be concerned, for in Alsace the French CP made an electoral alliance with the German Catholic autonomists.

The switch from "united front" to "class against class" inaugurated what came to be known in communist jargon as "the third period". At the world congress in the summer of 1928 Bukharin made a long and laboured effort to convince his hearers that the analysis of the world situation showed changes of such breadth and significance that a new policy was required to meet them. Social-democracy was no longer the right wing of the labour movement, but the left wing of the bourgeoisie. The congress theses argued that as social-democracy was becoming more bourgeois and imperialist, more and more an integral part of the bourgeois state, "the fight against bourgeois labour parties must be intensified".

Again the change coincided with a switch inside the USSR itself, where the policy of forced industrialization and the "liquidation of the kulaks as a class" was about to be launched. The connexion was made explicit by Manuilsky at the tenth ECCI plenum in the following year. "We never thought of the united front as a formula valid for all times and countries. There was a time when we negotiated with the Second and Two-and-a-half Internationals, with the General Council and Purcell. Now we are stronger and therefore use more aggressive methods in the struggle to win the majority of the working class." In the same way, the New Economic Policy had been a form of united front tactics with the individual peasants. To object to the new tactics, to the sharper attacks on social-democracy, was also to object to a sharper policy against the kulaks. "Whoever demands of us 'the maintenance of all norms of revolutionary legality' in regard to the kulaks will also have to preach loyalty to the trade union bureaucracy."

© JANE DEGRAS 1960

THE BOLSHEVISATION OF THE
SPARTACUS LEAGUE

By Richard Lowenthal

Introduction

WHEN THE Communist International was founded in March 1919, its declared purpose was to lead the working classes of the world to immediate revolution on the model of Bolshevik Russia. When the post-war crisis receded two years later, no proletarian revolution had taken place in any industrial country; yet the new organisation with its doctrine and its discipline persisted. The split in the international socialist movement, which had arisen from the first world war and the impact of the Bolshevik revolution, had become permanent.

For in the interval, Comintern had made a lasting imprint on the ideas and organisational forms of the revolutionary wing of the labour movement. As the parties of the Second International grew both larger and more reformist during the pre-war period, revolutionary minorities had continued to exist. Some of these professed Marxist, some syndicalist beliefs; some worked inside, some outside the "reformist" organisations. But all of them combined a belief in the revolutionary mission of the working class with emphasis on the international character of that mission; and nearly all, blaming the "burocratic degeneration" of the socialist mass parties and trade unions for their reformist policies, believed that victory for their own revolutionary trend depended on restoring complete democracy in the inner life of the movement.

Because of this, the Bolsheviks with their faith in centralist discipline had been distrusted rather than respected by the pre-1914 revolutionary Left. Rosa Luxemburg in particular, who was widely accepted in these circles as an interpreter of Russian revolutionary problems, took a definitely "Menshevik" view of the role and organisation of the socialist party. It was only during the war that Lenin's group emerged as the crystallising centre for the revolutionary wing of the socialist internationalists, the so-called Zimmerwald Left; and only their victory in Russia invested the Bolsheviks with the authority needed to make non-Russian revolutionaries listen seriously to their ideas of centralist organisation and dictatorship.

At the founding congress of Comintern, no more was asked of member parties than a willingness to support Soviet Russia, to fight in their own countries for a "proletarian dictatorship" based on Soviets, and to organise in separate parties without the "reformists". Only the Second World Congress in July 1920 laid down the famous 21 conditions for affiliation, which clearly aimed at the formation of a centralised world party based on Bolshevik principles of strategy and organisation. Their implementation required a complete transformation of the ideas and the inner life of each of the non-Russian member parties, as well as their effective subordination to a Russian-controlled centre. When, after years of factional conflicts and "purges", the process was at last completed, the remnants of the non-Leninist revolutionary Left had been reduced to the status of sectarian oddities. Instead of the pre-war split between a reformist majority and a revolutionary minority, both more or less democratic, the great division was now between a (increasingly reformist) democratic labour movement on one side, and the Communist parties organised for revolution on Bolshevik totalitarian principles on the other.

In what follows, we shall designate this transformation of democratic revolutionary parties into organs of the Leninist dictatorship by the convenient term of "Bolshevisation". In our view, the crucial stage of the process was the very first, when the Bolsheviks first set themselves this goal and learnt how to use their authority for achieving it. For a study of the factors that made Bolshevisation possible, the case of the German Communist Party is of outstanding interest, because it looked back to the autonomous revolutionary tradition of the Spartacus League and of Rosa Luxemburg's leadership, and because it was long to remain the most important non-Russian party in Comintern. Yet the crucial first phase in which the heir and defender of that tradition, Paul Levi, was defeated and Comintern's supremacy established lasted less than a year—from the Second World Congress in July 1920 to Levi's resignation from the leadership in February 1921, and to his expulsion after the "March Action".

The present paper does not claim to be more than a first sketch for such a "case study in Bolshevisation". Apart from published materials, I have also made use of some interviews with participants in the events described. But other valuable sources—notably the personal archive of

Paul Levi, now in a private collection in the United States—have had to be left unexplored for the present.

The Premature Party

The Spartacus League had been formed during the first world war by such leaders of the Revolutionary Marxist Left within German Social Democracy as Rosa Luxemburg, Franz Mehring and Klara Zetkin, together with Karl Liebknecht, who was not a Marxist but a passionate anti-militarist propagandist and became the first Reichstag member to vote against the war credits in defiance of party discipline. Its methods ranged from anti-war demonstrations (like the one on May 1st, 1916, which led to Liebknecht's arrest) to the circulation of secretly printed literature among the workers, where it supported strikes called in defiance of the official truce, and in the army; its main strongholds were in Wuerttemberg, in the Chemnitz area of Central Germany, in parts of the industrial Rhineland and in sections of the Greater Berlin organisation. The chief organiser of its underground work was Rosa Luxemburg's Polish compatriot and lifelong friend, Leo Jogiches-Tyszko.

The Spartacists aimed not merely at ending the war as quickly as possible by a "peace without annexations and indemnities", as did the "Social-Pacifists" of the later USPD (Independent Socialist Party), but like the Bolsheviks specifically regarded the war as an opportunity for revolution. Yet they differed from the Bolsheviks in not aiming at the creation of a separate revolutionary party. Lenin believed that the decision of most socialist parties to support their own country in the war was due to a "betrayal" by a few reformist leaders, backed by a "workers' aristocracy" corrupted with a share of the profits of colonial exploitation. From this he concluded that the revolutionaries everywhere must break with the traitors and form their own parties; and from his concept of a revolutionary party, developed in the Russian underground movement, it followed that they should separate not only from the "Social-Patriots" but also from the "Social-Pacifists".

But Rosa Luxemburg had rejected this concept of the revolutionary party as early as 1904[1] as based on an attempt to inject the "true" socialist consciousness into the labour movement by means of organisational devices. Her own concept of the party had always been that it could only express the actual views of the organised workers; if the latter were politically immature, the role of the Marxist was patiently

[1] Cf. Rosa Luxemburg in *Neue Zeit*, July 1904.

to enlighten them and to help them learn from experience, but never to try and impose on them the dictates of a self-appointed, infallible leadership. Of course, if reformist bureaucrats used undemocratic means to stop the workers from turning revolutionary, the critics might be *forced* to form their own party; but whenever possible it was preferable that the Communists, as Marx had advised, should *not* form a separate party. Accordingly, when in March 1917 the Independent Socialist Party was about to be formed, Rosa Luxemburg decisively rejected the idea that the existence of a pacifist and a revolutionary tendency made it necessary "to shepherd the workers into different, carefully separated party pens according to the tendencies within the opposition" as "based on a sectarian concept of the party".[2]

Yet that was the Bolshevik concept, and it was also advocated inside Germany by the followers of the Bremen weekly *Arbeiterpolitik*, later known as the *Internationale Kommunisten Deutschlands (IKD)*. Originally inspired by Karl Radek, but lacking nationally known leaders, this group was much smaller even than the Spartacist minority. But while the Spartacus League joined the USPD without renouncing its own propaganda, the *Arbeiterpolitik* called from May 1917 onwards for a separate party of the revolutionaries, and by July 1918, when the Bolsheviks were in power in Russia, had begun to "warn" the Spartacists that the Communist Party of Germany would be formed "with them or without them".[3]

When the Spartacus leaders emerged from the Kaiser's prisons in November 1918, events at once confirmed their view that conditions were not ripe for the formation of a new party. The first national congress of workers' and soldiers' councils, held in mid-December, showed that the overwhelming majority looked to the two socialist parties—the majority socialists and the Independents—who then formed the government; only 10 delegates out of 489 announced themselves as members of the Spartacus League.[4] But it also showed that the bulk of the USPD militants disapproved the policy of their representatives in the government: no less than 98 delegates voted against the government's plan to call early elections for a Constituent Assembly and in favour of maintaining "Soviet power", i.e. the rule of the Councils themselves, and this group included the Berlin revolutionary shop stewards who had led the metalworkers' strike of January

[2] *Der Kampf*, Duisburg, 31.III.1917, quoted by Paul Lange in *Freiheit*, Berlin, 26.IV.1921.   [3] Quoted by Lange, *ibid*.
[4] *Illustriente Geschichte der deutschen Revolution*, Berlin, 1928, pp. 249–50.

1918 and now controlled the Berlin Council.[5] Rosa Luxemburg and Jogiches concluded that their best hope was to unite all the supporters of "Soviet Power" by a joint struggle to change the policy of the USPD from within; hence they demanded an immediate USPD congress.[6]

Yet by Christmas the USPD leaders had replied that it was technically impossible to hold a congress before the elections to the Constituent Assembly. Moreover, Radek had arrived in Berlin with a mandate from the Bolshevik party, had attended a national conference of his friends, the *IKD*, and had persuaded them to offer the immediate formation of a joint party with the Spartacists.[7] In the circumstances Rosa Luxemburg agreed to propose to the Spartacus national conference on December 29th the creation of a new party on that basis, and the persistent doubts of Jogiches were overborne.

The very creation of the German Communist Party at this moment and in this improvised manner was thus partly the fruit of a successful Bolshevik intervention; and it resulted in a composition of the foundation congress which shocked the founders. Quite a few of the old Spartacus groups were not represented as they could not be reached in time; instead, many of the eighty-odd delegates represented new members without previous experience in the labour movement, ranging from young deserters from the army to revolutionary artists who had simply reacted to the upheaval of the time by joining the most extreme group. These people willingly re-elected the Spartacus leaders to head the new party, but did not follow their arguments; they applauded Rosa Luxemburg's speech expounding the programme, with its insistence that the party would "never take power except by the clear and unambiguous will of the great majority of the proletarian masses",[8] and then joined with the most sectarian of the old Spartacists in cutting the party off from that majority by deciding, against the leaders' advice, to boycott the forthcoming elections to the Constituent Assembly. That decision proved a powerful factor for the failure of negotiations with a delegation from the Berlin revolutionary shop stewards, who thus remained in the USPD as the core of its future "left wing". The leaders felt that the party had started prematurely and on the wrong foot: after the boycott decision, Jogiches

---

[5] *Ibid.*, p. 254.
[6] *Ibid.*, pp. 263–4; also Wilhelm Pieck, *Die Gruendung der KPD*, Berlin, n.d., p.24.
[7] *Ibid.*, p. 264.
[8] *Was will der Spartakusbund?*, Berlin, 1919, pp. 22–3.

urged once again that the attempt to form a party be abandoned,[9] and Rosa Luxemburg stated in one of her last letters that they ought to have made agreement on electoral participation a precondition of membership rather than submit to a chance vote.[10]

Within a few days, the young party got involved in a deadly clash with the government. The government's order deposing the police chief appointed by the Berlin Workers' Council had caused great excitement among the radical Berlin workers, but the Communist leaders decided, with Radek's approval, to avoid a trial of strength as the situation outside the capital was quite different. Yet at the crucial meeting with the Berlin shop stewards and local USPD officials, the Communist representatives, Liebknecht and Wilhelm Pieck, were carried away by the defiant mood of the crowd, and Liebknecht agreed to join a "Revolutionary Committee".[11] The aimless and leaderless January rising which thus began sealed the government's dependence on reactionary "Free Corps", and its defeat was followed by the capture and murder of Liebknecht and Luxemburg by Free Corps officers. During the following months, the radical workers suffered similar bloody defeats in a number of isolated strongholds, culminating in a second crushing of Berlin's militant Left in March and the killing of Jogiches.

Meanwhile the Constituent Assembly had begun its debates without any Communist voices, while a state of siege made other Communist propaganda all but impossible. Though the economic post-war troubles and hatred of the Free Corps drove a growing minority of the workers into opposition, the Communists, hardly visible as a party and with many of their best cadres killed or imprisoned, were not in a position to attract them, and only the USPD—large, legal and represented in parliament, and with strong radical elements that differed little from the Communists—profited. By the summer of 1919, it was thus clear that the future of the KPD depended on its ability to overcome its isolation from the mass of the radical workers, and to avoid further premature clashes with the armed forces. The surviving leaders soon came to realise that the solution of both problems might depend

[9] This was hinted at in *Illustrierte Geschichte*, p. 286, and made explicit by Paul Levi, in *Die Internationale*, II, 26, 1,XII.1920.

[10] Klara Zetkin in *Bericht ueber den 4. Parteitag der KPD (Sparatakusbund), 14. und 15. April 1920*, n.d.

[11] See *Illustrierte Geschichte*; also Radek, "Der Fall Levi", *Kommunistische Internationale*, Nr. 17, 1921, pp. 76–7, and Levi, *Was ist das Verbrechen?*, Berlin, 1921, pp. 33–4.

on correcting the false start into which they had been rushed—in other words, on a radical change in the composition of the party.

Though the Communist International had by then been founded (despite initial objections from the German delegate who had been mandated in this sense by Rosa Luxemburg and Jogiches), the Russian Bolsheviks, then in the most critical phase of their civil war, were not in a position to give advice. Radek kept in touch with the German party from a Berlin prison cell, but could intervene only indirectly. The Spartacus leaders were thus free to map a course of action for themselves; the task devolved primarily on Dr Paul Levi, who had taken over the leadership after Jogiches' death.

Paul Levi's political concept

As a young Frankfurt lawyer of left wing socialist views, Levi had met Rosa Luxemburg when defending her against a charge of *lèse-majesté* before the war, and had joined her circle. In the war he had been mobilised but later had managed to get to Switzerland; there he had made Lenin's acquaintance and had worked in the bureau of the Zimmerwald Left. He fell under the influence of Bolshevik ideas to the extent of supporting the formation of a separate revolutionary party; Lenin used him to work for a better understanding between the Spartacists and the Bremen *IKD*. He returned to Germany in time to take part in the underground work of the Spartacists before the November revolution; as a member of the new party's "Zentrale" (executive), he was one of the liaison men between it and Radek during the January rising.[12]

Levi's enemies, like Radek[13] and Ruth Fischer,[14] have described him as an aloof and arrogant intellectual, too vain to bear criticism, without contact with the workers and basically afraid of militant revolutionary action. The evidence certainly confirms that he was aloof and lonely, oversensitive to personal attacks and inclined to react with offers of resignation, and that his intellectual arrogance was greater than his ambition—a serious fault in a political leader. But against this we must hold Lenin's judgment uttered to Klara Zetkin at a time when Levi

[12] The biographical data about Levi have largely been taken from the hostile account of Radek, "Der Fall Levi".

[13] *Ibid.*

[14] *Stalin and German Communism*, Cambridge, Mass., 1948. This account has the interest due to an active and passionate participant in the events, but is not always reliable in its facts.

had already been expelled from the party, that "he has proved himself during the time of the worst persecutions, was brave, prudent, self-sacrificing".[15] In fact, the reason why not only his German colleagues, but the Russian leaders urged him to remain at the head of the party for months after conflicts had begun to manifest themselves was not only his undoubted intellectual superiority, but a rare political decisiveness rooted in moral courage and a marked sense of responsibility. It was precisely these qualities which made the breach inevitable in the end.

When Levi took charge of the KPD in March, 1919, he quickly realised that it would have been far better for the Spartacists to have followed Jogiches' advice and remained in the USPD for a few more months.[16] As it was, the revolutionary masses were supporting the USP, and the principal task of the prematurely founded KPD was to influence their development and to solidify the opposition of the USP "left wing" against leaders like Hilferding who had come to accept the constitutional basis of the parliamentary republic. But to win influence on the USP workers, most of whom were active trade unionists (during 1919, the left wing captured control of Germany's most important union, the metal workers), the Communists had to get rid of a syndicalist tendency in their own ranks which wanted to commit them to leaving the unions and founding new "revolutionary" unions instead. They also had to get rid of those elements who believed that the test of a good revolutionary was readiness to shoot it out with the government forces on every occasion, and who were therefore wide open to provocations.

During the summer of 1919, the party executive thus decided to dissolve the "Red Soldiers' League", which had transformed itself from a tool of Communist propaganda in the armed forces into a cluster of "Red Guard" units who defied the party's control.[17] Next, a party congress called in October to the Heidelberg area was faced with theses which insisted that the victory of the proletariat required the use of *all* political means—revolutionary or parliamentary—according to the situation, and that the economic struggle must be conducted by mass organisations which could not be artificially created; the

---

[15] Klara Zetkin, *Erinnerungen an Lenin*, Berlin-Wien, 1929, p. 32.

[16] Levi, *Berichte zum Zweiten Kongress der Kommunistischen Internationale*, Hamburg, 1921, pp. 21–35.

[17] Hugo Eberlein in *Bericht ueber den 3. Parteitag der KFD (Spartakusbund), 25. und 26. Feb. 1920*, and *Rote Fahne*, Nr. 593, 28.XII.21.

splitting of individual unions might become inevitable in the struggle against "bureaucratic traitors", but it could never become general Communist policy to leave the unions. The final thesis laid down that members who did not accept these principles could not remain in the party, and after it had been adopted with the narrowest of majorities, the opposing delegates were no longer admitted to the last day's session.[18]

The dissolution of the Red Soldiers' League has never been criticised inside the party even after Levi's fall. But many of the "fighting organisations" (KO) continued to exist secretly against the will of the leadership, whose decision they regarded as a betrayal of the revolutionary cause; and when the Heidelberg theses came to be discussed in the districts, they became the organised core of the opposition against them.[19] At the congress, Levi had concentrated his attack on the syndicalist views of two Hamburg intellectuals, Laufenberg and Wolffheim, and had thus sought to isolate the leading ideologues of the syndicalist trend. But as the debate developed in the organisations of an underground party with no regular press, the argument of the "leftist" opposition that Levi's real aim was to expel all true revolutionaries in order to form a parliamentary "coalition" with the USP seemed convincing to a large section of the rank and file. By the time of the next party congress in February 1920, most of the North German districts including Berlin had sided with the opposition; the total membership, officially counted as 106,000 at the Heidelberg congress and in fact lower even then, had been reduced by almost half.[20]

The errors of the foundation congress had been corrected at an extremely heavy cost. Yet there was a credit side to the picture: in December 1919, the Leipzig congress of the USPD showed marked successes for the left wing led by Ernst Daeumig of the Berlin revolutionary shop stewards. Under its pressure, the Congress adopted a programme favouring the dictatorship of the proletariat, broke with the Second International and called for negotiations with Comintern. This was the kind of development Levi had been working for: it

[18] The Theses in general were adopted by 31 : 18 votes, the last thesis enforcing the split only by 29 : 20, with six members of the party executive casting their votes in favour. *Bericht ueber den 2. Parteitag der KPD (Spartakusbund), 20–24. Okt. 1919*, n.d. The vote and split are on pp. 42–5, the final text of the theses on pp. 60–2.

[19] Eberlein at 3rd party congress and in *Rote Fahne*.

[20] Eberlein at 3rd party congress, pp. 33–8, and Heinrich Brandler, *ibid.*, p. 16.

seemed well worth while to lose some 30,000–40,000 semi-syndicalists, many of them without political experience and permanently un-employed, if there was a chance of winning the bulk of the 800,000 workers in the USP, who formed a majority of organised labour in Berlin, Central Germany and the Ruhr! Levi now believed this could be done, but not by trying to win them away from their party indi-vidually or in little groups, but by influencing the left wing leaders and helping them to gain control of their party as the Spartacists might have done if they had not prematurely broken away.[21]

Not even Levi's colleagues in the KPD executive understood this plan; indeed a number of them regarded the left wing leaders of the USP as equally bad with the right wing and likely to move forward only if "kicked hard".[22] But Levi's concept was wholly understood by Lenin. At first, the Bolshevik leader had been shocked at the news of the Heidelberg split; but by April 1920, when he wrote his book against *Left Wing Communism, an infantile disorder*, he declared that it was the duty of the German Communists to find a "compromise" with the left wing of the USP which would accelerate "the necessary com-plete fusion with this wing" without hampering the Communists in their ideological-political struggle against the right wing of the USP.[23]

Radek intervenes

No such approval for Levi's ideas, however, came from Karl Radek, who had in the meantime been released from German custody and taken up duty as secretary of Comintern. During the later part of his captivity, he had assisted the KPD's propaganda with a stream of pamphlets, but had found that his advice on internal party matters was not always equally welcome. He had agreed with the party executive on the need to fight syndicalist tendencies, and had written an open letter to the Heidelberg congress on these lines; but their decision to force a split on this issue took him by surprise, and he warned against it in a last-minute letter to Levi.[24] Yet Levi, feeling that this was his

[21] I have not found Levi's first comment on the Leipzig USP congress (referred to critically in *Bericht ueber den 3. Parteitag*, p. 15). But the ideas summarised in the text were consistently advocated by him in the debate at the 4th party con-gress, in his report to the Second World Congress of Comintern and in his comment in *Sowjet*, II, 3, Nov. 1920.

[22] Ernst Meyer at the 4th party congress, *Bericht*, p. 42.

[23] Lenin, *Selected Works*, Vol. X, London, 1938, pp. 114–15.

[24] Radek, "Der Fall Levi", p. 66.

responsibility and not Radek's, had gone ahead with the unanimous backing of the executive.

At this point, Radek's highly gifted, unscrupulous and strangely twisted personality becomes a factor in our story. He had begun his political career in the "Socialdemocratic Party of the Kingdom of Poland and Lituania" (SDKPL)—a revolutionary Marxist and passionately internationalist group, formed in opposition to the Polish nationalism of Pilsudski's PPS. Rosa Luxemburg and Jogiches were among the founders of the SDKPL, and kept a leading role in it long after they had settled in Germany. As part of the Russian Socialist underground movement, the SDKPL often had the casting vote in its factional quarrels; and at the end of 1911, when its leaders sided with the majority of Russian Socialists against Lenin, a Warsaw group that supported the Bolsheviks was expelled from the SDKPL. Among them was Radek.[25]

Radek's expulsion was complicated by a charge that he had "embezzled" party funds; and when he emigrated to Germany and began writing for SPD papers, the SDKPL protested that it was "intolerable that an individual expelled from a fraternal party for thieving should engage in public ostentatious activity in the German party".[26] Meanwhile Radek had been admitted to the Bremen branch and convinced it that the charges were unjustified, and after much public controversy, the SPD executive finally had to ask the Jena party congress of 1913 for a retroactive ruling that "persons expelled from fraternal parties for dishonourable reasons cannot be members of the SPD",[27] which was passed by a large majority.

I have not been able to go into the substance of these old charges, which may well have referred to nothing more shameful than a diversion of local funds to the expelled splinter group. What is certain is that the accusation bitterly rankled with Radek for many years afterwards, and left a deep and lasting animosity against Rosa Luxemburg, Jogiches and their circle.[28] As with his antagonist Levi, Radek's mordant irony acted as a carapace to a highly vulnerable ego; but while Levi tended to retire when hurt, Radek's sensitivity was of the perverse

[25] For a brief account of this Polish pre-war split see Bertram Wolfe, *Three who made a Revolution*, London, 1956, pp. 519–20; also M. K. Dziewanowski, *The Communist Party of Poland*, Cambridge (Mass.), 1959, p. 52.

[26] *Protokoll des Jenaer Parteitages der SPD 1913*, Berlin, 1913, p. 537.

[27] *Ibid.*, p. 536, and pp. 543–4.

[28] Cf. the USP editor W. Herzog on his talks with Radek; the Munich *Forum*, IV, 11, Aug. 1920, pp. 808–9; IV, 12, Sept. 1920, p. 901.

kind that delights in displaying its wounds. The very pseudonym he chose served as a constant reminder of his humiliation: its abbreviation was K. Radek, and Kradek is Polish for thief.

Finally, though Radek had early thrown in his lot with the Bolsheviks and had worked closely with Lenin, his status in the Russian party was insecure: he never became a member of its Central Committee. The Bolsheviks chiefly esteemed him as an expert on the German movement, and had sent him to Berlin at the first opportunity. The KPD was to some extent his creation, and his urge to prove himself as their guide to true Bolshevik tactics must have been overwhelming.

Yet while Radek was powerless in his cell, the collective of Rosa Luxemburg's disciples had not only defied his advice, but had virtually undone his work of the founding days and recreated a homogeneous party according to their ideas. Even apart from any drive towards centralisation of authority inherent in Bolshevik ideology and the institution of Comintern, Radek thus had strong personal motives for looking askance at the autonomy and cohesion of the Spartacus leadership; and once installed in Moscow, he endeavoured to break up the team's solidarity, to counterbalance it with outside elements, and to discredit its leader.

His first move was an attack on Levi for his exaggerated "anti-Putschism". Writing about the role of Eugen Leviné and the Munich Communists who had joined the Bavarian "Soviet Republic" although they had had no share in creating it, and had fallen for a cause they knew to be hopeless rather than abandon the fighting masses, Levi had raised a doubt whether such heroic sacrifice was really the best service Communists could render in similar circumstances. That gave Radek his cue: in his preface to a pamphlet on the related experience of the Hungarian Soviet Republic, he poured scorn on "political raisonneurs" who thought the Communists should never fight without a "certified guarantee of victory".

Though Levi's name was not mentioned, the target of Comintern's new secretary was obvious to every reader when the preface was published in the KPD's theoretical journal, *Die Internationale*.[29] Levi replied that he had doubted not the need for revolutionaries to risk all in great national crises, but the usefulness of getting drawn into isolated local clashes where defeat was certain. The Communists, he urged, should have the courage to serve the masses not only by spurring them on

[29] Vol. II, Nr. 21. I have not been able to consult this issue.

in promising situations, but also by holding them back in hopeless ones.[30]

Meanwhile, however, Radek had gained some support for his attack from differences that had arisen among the KPD leaders over the party's policy at the time of the Kapp Putsch—the military coup of March 1920 which had been defeated by a general strike proclaimed by the trade unions in cooperation with the legal government. These differences did not concern the party executive's failure to support the general strike from the start and to call the workers to arms: the gravity of this mistake, first criticised by Levi in a passionate letter from the prison where he was kept all through the Putsch, was generally admitted.[31]   The dispute turned on the party's famous offer of "loyal opposition" to a "socialist government", made when after the defeat of the coup the formation of such a government had been proposed to the USP by the trade union leaders, and when the USP hesitated from fear of attacks from the Left.[32] When Levi emerged from prison a few days afterwards, he had approved the substance of this offer and only criticised its clumsy wording;[33] Lenin later expressed the same view in a postscript to his book on left wing Communism.[34] But a majority of the fourth party congress in April condemned the whole offer as opportunist.

Now Paul Froelich, the only representative of Radek's former Bremen pupils in the party executive, made this dispute the basis for a general attack on Levi's leadership. In an article published on the eve of Comintern's Second World Congress, he claimed in defiance of the facts that the offer had been *inspired* by Levi, and that chances of further revolutionary action had been sacrificed to his longing for a respite in which the party could peacefully educate the workers. But the masses would never become ready for revolution "in the Marvist school-room", only by action. The formula in the Spartacus programme that

---

[30] "Die Lehren der ungarischen Revolution", *Die Internationale*, II, 24, June 24, 1920.

[31] See *Kommunisticheskii International*, Nr. 12, July 20, 1920, cols. 2077–80, quoted in E. H. Carr, *The Bolshevik Revolution*, III, London, 1953, p. 174 n.; also Levi in *Bericht ueber den 5. Parteitag der KPD (Sektion der Kommunistischen Internationale)*, 4–.5. *Nov. 1920*, Berlin, 1921, p. 35.

[32] Nrs. II, 23–5, of *Die Internationale* (June 1st, June 24th and July 24th, 1920), Nr. 12 of *Kommunisticheskii International* of July 20, 1920, and *Die Lehren des Kapp-Putsches* by M. J. Braun, Leipzig, 1920.

[33] Levi at the 4th KPD congress, *Bericht*, pp. 48–50.

[34] *Selected Works*, Vol. X, pp. 150–2.

the Communists would only take power with the explicit consent of the great majority of the workers was liable to dangerous misreadings, Froelich wrote; in Levi's hands it had become "castrated" and turned into a means to prevent or weaken action.[35] What here emerged was the germ of a factional platform, advocating minority action as a means of "educating" the masses—as well as the germ of the legend that Levi had prevented effective revolutionary action at the time of the Kapp Putsch.

The occasion for Radek's second move came when the "left wing Communists" who had left the KPD after Heidelberg founded a new "Communist Workers Party" (KAPD) early in April and applied for affiliation to Comintern. It was natural that Comintern, even while rejecting the anti-parliamentary and anti-trade union platform of the Leftists, should try to keep in friendly contact in order to influence them; after all, they claimed 38,000 members—not much less than were left in the KPD—and remained much stronger than the official party in Berlin and Hamburg. After prolonged discussion with two KAPD emissaries, Comintern thus on June 2nd addressed an open letter to the new group which gently reasoned with them about their errors, urged them to expel Laufenberg, Wolffheim and Ruehle (the last-named had criticised the party dictatorship in Russia), and invited them to send delegates to the forthcoming world congress on the understanding that they would submit in advance to its decisions.[36]

But Comintern went beyond these obvious points in stressing that, while generally supporting the KPD against the leftist rebels, it was "completely out of agreement with the reasons given by the Spartacus executive in its well-known statement of 21 March, 1921, on the possibility of forming a 'purely socialist government'". Now only three weeks before, Lenin had written that "the basic premise and the practical conclusions of that statement are quite correct", though its formulation was not;[37] but the KAPD attacked not only the formulation, but the whole policy. By officially disavowing the formulation without defending the policy itself, the Comintern letter deliberately took up a position of mediation between the two parties and of encouragement for left wing critics within the KPD. Even more

[35] Froelich, "Die Kappiade und die Haltung der Partei", in *Die Internationale*, II, 24, June 24, 1920.

[36] *The Communist International 1919–1943, Documents* (ed. Jane Degras), Vol. I, London, 1956 (hereafter cited as *Documents* ed. Degras), pp. 94–9.

[37] See note 34 above.

striking was the suggestion that KAPD and KPD should at once agree on a joint provisional organisation bureau, with a member of Comintern's executive as chairman with the casting vote; for this implied that in the interest of unity, the authority of Comintern was to be substituted for that of the Spartacus leaders.

The letter had no immediate practical consequences, for the KAPD at that time refused either to expel the ideologues named by Moscow, to submit in advance to the decisions of the forthcoming world congress, or to approach the KPD for cooperation. Meanwhile, however, a third source of disagreement between Comintern and KPD had arisen over the vital issue of the USPD.

At the Leipzig USPD congress, the left wing had demanded unconditional affiliation to Comintern; the reluctant right wing had proposed "negotiations with Comintern and other social-revolutionary parties" as a compromise, and got it adopted. Comintern had replied with a letter recounting all the political sins of the right wing leaders, rejecting any negotiation about "a new international", and inviting the USPD to send delegates to Moscow in order to discuss the terms of affiliation with Comintern and fusion with the KPD.[38] When the USPD leaders neither answered nor published this letter, it was published in Germany by Comintern's West European secretariat, and a reminder sent in May.[39] But by June, when official invitations went out calling the Second World Congress for July 15, the USPD still had not issued the original letter to its members. Radek now proposed to ECCI to call on all local and regional USPD organisations to elect delegates to the Congress directly over the head of their leaders, and this appeal went out on June 21:[40] he was now convinced that there was no more chance for collective affiliation as the left wing leaders would not fight for it, and that the best hope was to break loose individual groups. But Levi, by then in confidential contact with the left wing leaders, kept working for collective fusion.

Comintern's Second Congress

When the KPD delegation arrived at the Second World Congress, there were thus two tactical disputes pending between it and ECCI—on relations with the USPD and the KAP—in addition to the open personal feud between its leader and the secretary of Comintern. But

[38] *Documents* ed. Degras, pp. 74–80. [39] *Ibid.*, pp. 92–3.
[40] Herzog diary, *Forum*, IV, 12, Sept. 1920, pp. 871–5; *Documents* ed. Degras, p. 100.

this did not necessarily mean then, as it would have meant in later times, that Levi was "in disgrace" in Moscow; for Lenin, who could only intermittently devote his attention to Comintern affairs, was not committed in either dispute, and Levi enjoyed his full political confidence. Yet when the Congress ended one month later, this confidence had been shaken, and Radek could go ahead in forming a left wing faction against Levi on the basis of genuine differences of principle.

The reason for this change, which turned "Bolshevisation" from a personal dream of Radek's into an official policy of Comintern backed by the Russian leadership, is closely linked to the major international event which dominated the Congress—the Soviet offensive in Poland. The fact that the Soviet government had not only survived intervention and civil war, but was advancing victoriously into Europe, served greatly to increase the Bolsheviks' authority. Already Lenin's book on *Left Wing Communism* had started from the assumption that the history of the Bolshevik party was the model from which all revolutionary socialists had to learn; now at the Congress, that assumption was made the basis of the new conditions of affiliation to Comintern.

But if the Polish campaign increased the Bolsheviks' international authority, it equally increased their dependence on international working class action geared to their specific needs. When, on the very eve of the congress, Lenin decided to reject the British offer of mediation and to continue the offensive towards Warsaw, he had been deliberately taking the risk of renewed allied intervention in the hope that the Red Army's advance would bring revolution not only to Poland, but to Germany and all Central Europe. True, there were diplomatic contacts between Russia and the bourgeois German government;[41] in return for the German refusal to let Allied supplies for Poland pass through, Germany's hope of recovering the "Polish Corridor" had to be kept alive. But this was just a short-term reinsurance—the real question was how soon the German workers would rise if Russian troops appeared at the frontier. Angelica Balabanoff, who attended the congress as a member of the Russian delegation, reports that a sceptical reply of Levi's to this question—"perhaps after months, perhaps not at all"—given privately to Lenin, was the beginning of his downfall.[42] But there exists more official evidence on the matter.

[41] Cf. Carr, *The Bolshevik Revolution*, III, p. 327–8.
[42] In a letter to the present writer.

Lenin delivered the opening report to the Congress on the Fundamental Tasks of Comintern. But neither he nor any other speaker referred publicly to a vital last-minute change in the theses he was presenting. In Lenin's original draft, dated July 4, Thesis 5 had stated that "the task of the moment for the Communist parties is *not* to accelerate revolution, but to accelerate the work of preparing the proletariat".[43] In the final text adopted by the Congress, it said on the contrary that "the task of the moment is *now* to accelerate the revolution, without provoking it by artificial means before adequate preparation has taken place", and added: "The preparation of the proletariat for the revolution must be promoted by action." [44] In reporting the change to the fifth congress of the KPD, Ernst Meyer stated explicitly that it had been made because of the "acute revolutionary situation" created by the offensive against Warsaw;[45] more than a year later, he disclosed that Paul Levi had opposed the change in the commission of the Congress.[46]

We may safely date the first change in the Russian leaders' attitude to Levi from that refusal to subordinate the timing of revolutionary action to Russian needs. Lenin himself did not cling to this concept after it had failed in Poland—but by then the whole ideology and organisation of Comintern had been geared to it.

The Russian belief in an acute revolutionary situation also changed the framework in which their attitude to the KAPD was decided.[47] Granted that this leftist splinter represented a syndicalist rather than a Marxist current—were not syndicalists and even anarchists potential allies in a revolutionary crisis? There was to be no concession to syndicalism in the ideology and tactics of the Communist parties themselves, as laid down by the Congress, yet the syndicalists were to be welcomed as comrades in action—their prejudices would be overcome in the practice of the common struggle.[48]

This reasoning was promptly applied to the KAPD. Whether the Russians really believed that it represented "revolutionary masses" that could not otherwise be reached, or whether they were chiefly interested in the fact that most of the former military cadres of the

[43] *Selected Works*, Vol. X, 166–7. Italics ours.

[44] *Protokoll des 2. Weltkongresses der Kommunistischen Internationale*, Hamburg, 1920, pp. 751–2. Italics ours.

[45] *Bericht ueber den 5. Parteitag*, p. 118.

[46] "Ueber Offensivtaktik", *Rote Fahne*, Nr. V/37, Jan. 22, 1922.

[47] See Ernst Meyer's account in *Bericht ueber den 5. Parteitag*, p. 125.

[48] Cf. particularly Trotsky's speech in *Protokoll des 2. Weltkongresses*, p. 91 sqq.

KPD had joined these Leftists,[49] the Russians proposed to ignore their refusal to submit in advance to Congress decisions and to admit their delegates to the Congress, at first without voting rights and finally, when the KAP delegates hesitated to accept that, even with full voting rights. When the KPD delegates heard of this intention to give the expelled Leftists equal status with the orthodox party, they wrote to the Russians asking for a chance to explain their objections to their Central Committee, as the matter was of "vital" importance to the German party; and when refused a hearing, the Germans even told the Russians that they would leave the Congress if such a decision was taken. Nevertheless it was taken,[50] though by then even Radek felt that this was putting too high a premium on refusal to accept majority decisions; the French syndicalist Rosmer reports in his memoirs that Radek spoke in the ECCI meeting against the motion of the Russian delegation, and that this breach of discipline was the reason why he was not then re-elected secretary of Comintern.[51] The drama ended farcically: the KAPD delegates finally declined to take their seats, and the KPD delegation stayed on. But Levi remained deeply disturbed that the Russians had decided an important matter affecting the German movement without even hearing him, and the Russians were angry at the threat to depart: they discerned in it a continuing reserve against their "leading role", hailing from Rosa Luxemburg's influence,[52] and though the German delegation's threat had been unanimous, they blamed Levi for it.

Finally, the same difference of approach showed itself, if less bitterly, on a far more important issue: the handling of the USPD and, more generally, the conditions of affiliation to Comintern. The USPD had, after all, sent an official delegation; but both Crispien and Dittmann of the right wing and Daeumig and Stoecker of the left wing had arrived with a common desire to join Comintern, but to preserve the unity and autonomy of their party. On one side, all of them at least partly defended the USPD'S record. On the other hand, even the right wing delegates were willing to subscribe to all kinds of conditions embodying the principles of Communism in order to avoid a split in their party—but they clearly had not become Communists. Similar "cen-

[49] See notes 17 and 19 above.

[50] The whole wrangle is retold by Meyer and Levi in *Bericht ueber den 5. Parteitag*, pp. 27–9 and 36.
Parteitag", pp. 27–9 and 36.

[51] Rosmer, *Moscou sous Lenine*, Paris, 1953, pp. 116–18.

[52] Meyer in *Bericht ueber den 5. Parteitag*, p. 27.

trist" mass parties—parties that were neither consistently reformist nor Communist—at the time showed a similar tendency in France and Italy: they wished to join the International led by the victorious Russian Bolsheviks and yet retain their traditional character. For the Bolsheviks in turn the problem was how to avoid being used as a "cover" by the "unprincipled opportunist leaders" of these parties, and yet to win the mass of their "honest workers" who wished to become Communists, but to do so within their traditional parties!

According to Bolshevik doctrine, the only solution was to split these parties and expel the right wing leaders; hence the reluctance of the USPD left wing leaders to face a split caused a great deal of uncertainty and division in both the Russian and German Communist delegations. To Radek and Ernst Meyer, it seemed clear that nothing was to be hoped from the left wing leaders either, that collective affiliation was therefore chimerical, and that nothing remained to do but to force piecemeal breakaways.[53] But most of the Russian leaders were loath to forego the chance of a much quicker increase of influence by collective affiliation—if that could be achieved with adequate safeguards. After much debate behind the scenes, they finally decided to leave the door open but to strengthen the safeguards. The number of conditions of affiliation was raised from the original 18 to 21, the list of leaders specifically to be excluded was lengthened to name Hilferding in particular, and the expulsion of all delegates to the forthcoming party congresses who would oppose these terms was demanded; moreover, no party was to be admitted unless two-thirds of the members of their leading organs were people who had supported unconditional affiliation before the World Congress.[54] As this tightening up of conditions (in which Lenin himself took an active part) proceeded, accompanied by a chorus of denunciations of the right wing and disquisitions about the need for a split, the USPD delegation broke under the pressure: before the Congress ended, Daeumig and Stoecker had publicly declared that they would work for the acceptance of all conditions and fusion with the KPD.[55]

In one sense, this outcome was a triumph for Levi over Radek and the critics in his own party. For many months, he had worked consistently for collective affiliation of the USPD, to be achieved by an understanding with its left wing leaders, and now this hope was going

[53] *Protokoll des 2. Weltkongresses*, pp. 298 (Meyer) and 400 (Radek).

[54] See Meyer's commission report, *ibid.*, pp. 656–8.

[55] *Ibid.*, p. 372.

to come true. Yet as the debate proceeded, he was filled with forebodings which he finally was driven to hint at in public session.[56] He was sceptical about the legalistic formulation of 18 paragraphs, he said —that was not the way to rally the masses of USPD workers. Yet what mattered was to make the issues clear before the masses, not simply to split the organisation. The concept in Levi's mind was that a revolutionary mass party could not be created by forcing a split on organisational conditions, but by putting forward a policy which the USPD workers would approve but which all non-revolutionary elements would have to oppose: if that was done, the right wing leaders did not have to be expelled in advance, but would be forced to isolate themselves and would lose their influence. It was a way of thinking as fundamentally in conflict with the Bolshevik concept of the party as it was in line with the thought of Rosa Luxemburg: the 21 conditions mark the point when Levi, who had developed under both influences, recognised the need for a choice.

Levi's forebodings proved justified when the splitting of the USPD was carried out according to Bolshevik rules at its Halle congress in October 1920. After an historic debate, in which Zinovyev and the freshly exiled Menshevik leader Martov acted as protagonists for the opposing sides, the 21 conditions were accepted by 236 votes against 156. But not only did most of the USPD's parliamentary representatives and newspapers remain with the "right wing leaders"; many of the rank and file failed to understand the need for a split caused by no revolutionary crisis in Germany but by organisational demands from abroad. In the end, out of a total of 800,000 members only about 300,000 joined the Communists,[57] and most of these were post-war recruits with little experience in the labour movement.[58]

The greatest offence was caused by the language of the conditions concerning trade union work. These called not only for the forming of party "cells" within the unions, but demanded that these should fight to make their unions break with the "yellow" Amsterdam Inter-

[56] *Protokoll des 2. Weltkongresses*, pp. 361–2.

[57] *Documents* ed. Degras, p. 196. The number of KPD members at the time of fusion is given there as below 50,000, but the report to the 5th party congress lists more than 78,000 for Oct. 1, *Bericht*, p. 5.

[58] In spring, 1921, Radek admitted that the "overwhelming majority" of the pre-split social-democrats were still in SPD and USPD, while the "overwhelming majority" of the Communist rank and file had been aroused to political activity only by war and revolution. Radek, *Soll die VKPD eine Massenpartei der revolutionaeren Aktion oder eine zentristische Partei des Wartens sein?*, Hamburg, 1921.

national and affiliate with the newly founded Red International of Labour Unions (Profintern) instead. In Germany, where the unions had on the whole preserved their unity despite all the splits in the political movement, this shocked many of the radical union militants. Coupled with the total lack of feeling for this mood shown in Halle by Zinovyev and Lozovsky, the chief of Profintern, this cost the Communists the chance of capturing the leadership of the metal-workers' union: the team of militant workers who had been the backbone of the anti-war opposition and of later pro-Soviet feeling in this vital union, and who had taken control of it in the previous year, was broken up over this issue, and only a minority joined Comintern.

Comintern builds a Faction

Levi's resistance to the new formula about "accelerating the revolution", his sharp opposition to the courting of the KAPD and his doubts about the magic political effect ascribed to splits over organisational conditions—all coming at the moment when the Bolsheviks were confidently setting out to reorganise Comintern in their own image—could not fail to stamp him as an obstacle to their plans. The Russian leaders now reacted by backing with their full authority in private conversations those criticisms of KPD policy which Radek had first developed in his quarrel with Levi. The Spartacus leaders had not only unjustified reserves against their Russian comrades, it was now said; they had far too little "contact with the masses", and their obsessive fear of Putsches tended to paralyse their will to action. It could only be healthy if Comintern could induce the KAP to join in the forthcoming party fusion as a third partner, as the revolutionary *élan* of the "left wing Communists" might then balance the passivity of the Spartacus leaders and the opportunism of the USPD.[59]

But the Russians also hinted that not all the KPD leaders were equally to blame: there obviously was a "right wing", led by Levi, and a "left wing", represented e.g. by Meyer and Froelich. Levi tended to brush aside such talk, but Meyer did not. The Russians implied that they did not think the left wing was free from faults, but just then the chief mistakes were due to the right.[60] In short, they were trying to create a situation where they could balance two wings inside the KPD leadership, just as they were preparing to hold the balance between KAPD, KPD and left wing USPD.

[59] See Meyer's account to the 5th KPD congress, *Bericht*, pp. 27–8.
[60] *Ibid.*, p. 26.

The main spadework was once again left in Radek's hands. The fact that he had been demoted for partly siding with the Germans on the KAP issue, and that he was at heart as sceptical about immediate revolutionary possibilities as Levi—he had advised against the attack on Warsaw[61]—only increased his psychological need to prove his superior loyalty to the Russian Central Committee. He himself disclosed later that at the Congress he had assured Ernst Meyer of his conviction that the latter would never leave "the party"; with Levi, he had told Meyer even then, he was not so sure, but Levi would still be needed—"particularly for agitation in the Reichstag"—until better leaders had grown up.[62] Nor were Radek's faction-building efforts confined to old Communists: the left wing USPD editor Wilhelm Herzog, who during the Congress had favoured Radek's idea of breaking up the USPD rather than working for collective affiliation, left Moscow strongly primed against Levi's "opportunism",[63] and with a mandate to prepare an anti-Levi group among the left wing USPD-ers, which was after the fusion to cooperate with corresponding elements in the KPD.[64]

Levi was aware of most of these manœuvres, and he left the congress feeling that the misgivings expressed by Rosa Luxemburg and Jogiches about a Bolshevik-led International had been prophetic.[65] But when soon afterwards the Red Army was defeated before Warsaw and Lenin recognised the new situation by concluding an armistice with Poland, he thought that the main cause of the dispute had disappeared. Hence when the 5th congress of the KPD met at the beginning of November to prepare for fusion, he made no mention of his opposition to the Moscow formula about "accelerating the revolution" which now seemed as outdated as were the past differences on relations with the USPD. As a gesture to Russian susceptibilities, the KPD executive even dropped the memory of the Spartacus League from the party's name without awaiting the merger: in its former place in brackets, it now described itself as "section of the Communist International".

Nevertheless, an open clash between Comintern and the KPD executive developed at this very congress on the one remaining issue

[61] Cf. Carr, *The Bolshevik Revolution*, III, p. 209.
[62] Radek, "Der Fall Levi", *Kommunistische Internationale*, Nr. 17, 1921, p. 67.
[63] See Herzog's diary, *Forum*, V, 7, April 1921, pp. 275, 278.
[64] Interview Kurt Geyer.
[65] Herzog diary, *Forum*, V, 7, April 1921, p. 278. Also interviews Heinrich Brandler, Kurt Geyer.

—the need for overtures to the KAPD, though the latter's importance was now clearly declining. In the meantime the KAPD, while maintaining its basic positions, had purged itself of the three ideologues whose expulsion Moscow had demanded, and had applied for admission to Comintern as a "sympathising" party. Zinovyev, after talking with their leaders in Berlin, had hinted to the KPD that this "sympathising" status might be granted;[66] in an open letter to the KPD congress, he urged that the KAPD's good working class elements must be won "at any price" for the new united party.[67]

To this, Levi replied that the effort must be made but not at the price of ideological concessions.[68] In secret session, he added a warning that Comintern should not confuse the search for allies in the worldwide struggle against imperialism with the formation of Communist parties. As allies, syndicalists and anarchists could be as valuable as the revolutionary nationalists in the colonies; as Communists they could not be recognised unless they changed their ideas.[69] At once, the Comintern representative rose to protest: clear Communist parties could not be created by concentrating on ideological schooling "until the party had grey hairs on its superclever head", but only by mass struggles which required cooperation with all kinds of mass organisations, including syndicalist ones.[70] The relevance of this argument to the tiny KAPD was not clear, but the charge of lack of revolutionary activity had now been officially made by a Comintern spokesman before a party congress. It was echoed in public session by a motion of the Hamburg district which accused the party's Reichstag "group", i.e. Levi and Klara Zetkin, of failure to arouse the masses by revolutionary speeches;[71] the motion was voted down, but not before the mover, Hugo Urbahns, had blurted out that it was "being supported by the Third International"![72] Comintern's faction-building was now on the record.

Levi reacted to the attack by seeking to regain the confidence of the Russian leaders over the heads of the Comintern *apparachiki*. By the end of November, Lenin was telling the Bolsheviks that the European revolution had slowed down, but that Soviet Russia would gain a breathing space by playing on the conflicts between the imperialists

---

[66] Reported at the 5th KPD congress by Meyer and Stoecker, *Bericht*, pp. 29 and 35.

[67] *Ibid.*, p. 62. [68] *Ibid.*, p. 87.

[69] *Ibid.*, pp. 36–7. [70] *Ibid.*, p. 41.

[71] *Ibid.*, p. 93. [72] *Ibid.*, p. 107.

and allying herself with the oppressed nations.[73] Levi had been opposed to the idea of "accelerating" the German revolution in response to a Russian military offensive, but he was as willing as ever to defend the Russian revolution against any renewal of intervention, as he was convinced that large masses of workers would regard such intervention as an attack on themselves. In line with Lenin's new concept, he centred his programmatic speech to the fusion congress at the beginning of December on the vision of Russia as a world power, based on the support of the oppressed classes and nations everywhere. Russia was the head of a world-wide movement, and if the allied powers reached out again to destroy this head, it was the duty of the new party to act as its protective arm.[74]

Yet Radek who had reappeared as Comintern delegate at this congress continued to support from behind the scenes a concept of the revolutionary offensive which Lenin had clearly discarded. Ernst Meyer, who had lately been working in Comintern's "Little Bureau" in Moscow, specially stressed the party's duty to support Russia actively "even if Russia's defensive war against capitalist states is transformed into a military offensive".[75] More significant, Levi's draft of a manifesto for the united party was rejected as insufficient by the KPD executive under Radek's influence; in its place, a text of Radek's which the executive had not even seen was introduced into the congress at the last moment and adopted without debate![76] The crucial passage in this text stated that

> "while a party to which only tens of thousands listen may recruit its followers primarily by propaganda, a party whose organisation comprises hundreds of thousands and to which millions are listening must recruit primarily by deeds, by action. . . . The United Communist Party has strength enough to go into action on its own whenever events allow or require it." [77]

This was a clear, programmatic sanction for minority action, and it was bound to prove all the more explosive because the new members from the USPD were eager to see revolutionary action now they had

[73] E.g. speech before the Moscow nuclei secretaries, 26.XI.20; *Selected Works*, VIII, pp. 282–90.

[74] *Bericht ueber die Verhandlungen des Vereinigungsparteitages*, Berlin, 1921, pp. 31, 36–8.

[75] *Ibid.*, p. 55.

[76] Ernst Friesland (Ernst Reuter), *Zur Krise unserer Partei*, Berlin, 1921, p. 21 n.

[77] *Bericht ueber den Vereinigungsparteitag*, p. 232.

come under the authentic revolutionary leadership of Comintern. But the new mass party still represented very much a minority of the working class;[78] and the workers in general were becoming less, and not more, willing to fight as the post-war inflationary boom gave way to growing unemployment and more and more strikes were being lost.

In the circumstances, Levi had rather better reasons than on previous occasions to offer his resignation. But the colleagues who had just over-ruled him on policy still wanted him to continue as leader, and Radek, too, considered him indispensable for making the two components of the new united party grow together, if only because he enjoyed the personal confidence of the outstanding leaders of the USPD left wing. Under their moral pressure, he finally yielded and was unanimously elected joint chairman of the VKPD with Ernst Daeumig of the USPD.[79]

The leaders of the new party learnt only several weeks later from the KAPD press that the ECCI had, on the very eve of their fusion congress, decided to admit the KAPD as a "sympathising party"— though in doing so it had explained that the new VKPD would be the only regularly affiliated German section of Comintern, and that sym-pathising status was being granted to the KAP only temporarily in the hope of further fusion.[80] The gesture was obviously futile as by then the KAP had only some 20,000 members left compared to the 300,000–400,000 of the VKPD, but continued to hurl abuse at the latter; it only made sense as one of Comintern's means for goading the new party into a more "offensive" policy. Hence when the VKPD reacted to the news with a public protest,[81] Zinovyev caused ECCI to reject the challenge to its authority,[82] while Radek commented tartly in the VKPD's own paper on the "social democratic dislike of some leaders for any not fully enlightened revolutionary worker",[83] and told his left wing friends that Comintern would have no need to bother about the KAP if its official section conducted a more "active" policy.[84]

[78] At the Prussian elections of Feb. 1921, the Communists obtained 1,211,000 votes compared with 4,294,000 for the SPD and 1,075,000 for the remnant of the USP.

[79] Radek, "Der Fall Levi", *Kommunistische Internationale*, Nr. 17, 1921, p. 67.

[80] *Documents* ed. Degras, p. 206.

[81] *Rote Fahne*, Berlin, Nr. III/270, 28.XII.20.

[82] See *Kommunistische Internationale*, Nr. 16, 1921, pp. 431–3.

[83] *Rote Fahne*, Nr. III/271, 29.XII.20.

[84] See e.g. Ernst Friesland (Reuter), "Wir und die KAPD", *Rote Fahne*, Nr. IV/39 of 25.I.21.

By the turn of the year at the latest, it must thus have been obvious to Levi that Comintern would not desist from its efforts to undermine the cohesion of the party leadership and his personal influence, and that it was in a favourable position for doing so. Radek had been fairly successful in playing on differences even among the pre-fusion Communist leaders, and the executive of the new party was of course less homogeneous and less linked by common experience of danger than the old Spartacus team. They were now leading a mass party, and Levi was not the type of a popular mass leader. Above all, his grand design for fusing the small core of trained Spartacists with the unschooled revolutionary masses of the USPD had reached fulfilment largely thanks to the attraction of Moscow for these masses, and at a moment when they were being increasingly isolated from the main force of the German working class by the contrast between their own revolutionary impatience and the declining possibilities of revolutionary action. In the circumstances, it was foreseeable that this very fulfilment might become the prelude to his downfall.

Yet there was one important factor that could still save him: the growing divergence between the analysis of the world situation and the policies based on it by the responsible Russian leaders on one side, and by Comintern on the other. During this winter of 1920/21 the Bolsheviks were passing through the critical transition from "War Communism" at home and revolutionary offensive abroad to the New Economic Policy and to a foreign policy of "peaceful co-existence", founded on manœuvres to divide their enemies. But while Lenin was drawing the lessons from the failure of the Polish campaign as well as from victory in the civil war and looking to a breathing space, Comintern was still busy defending the "principle" of the revolutionary offensive[85] and prodding its sections accordingly. Sooner or later, the "contradiction" was bound to be solved; for in the framework of Lenin's new policy, it was clearly preferable that the foreign Communist parties should be capable of supporting the Soviet state by broadly-based mass movements even in non-revolutionary situations, rather than that they should isolate themselves from the bulk of the workers in vain attempts to seize power by minority action.

At the beginning of 1921, few German Communists were aware of these divergences: the habit of studying Russian party discussions in order to adjust one's line in advance to the prevailing trend was not

[85] E.g. N. Bukharin, "Ueber die Offensivtaktik", *Kommunistische Internationale*, Nr. 15, 1921.

yet part of the professional equipment of a Communist leader. Among the few, however, were Levi on one side and some of Radek's "left" pupils in the party's Berlin district leadership on the other; and they drew opposite conclusions from it. Levi accepted Lenin's analysis as realistic and corresponding to the best interests of the international movement as well; he based on it a hope that the Russian leaders would in due course correct the lag in Comintern's "ideological superstructure", and a willingness to prove by deeds the usefulness of a broad mass party to the young Soviet state. Conversely, the young leaders of the "Berlin Left", notably Ruth Fischer and the Russian-born Arkady Maslow, felt that Soviet foreign policy was tending to sacrifice the interests of world revolution to Russia's need for a breathing space, and that speedy revolutionary action was needed in order to help Zinovyev as head of Comintern to oppose this "opportunist" trend. In their minds, the fight against Levi thus became part of the wider struggle against the danger of Soviet opportunism.[86]

The person for whom this constellation was most embarrassing was Radek. Far more intelligent than Zinovyev, he could see the force of Lenin's (and Levi's) estimate of the situation, and realised that the usefulness of the movement to Soviet Russia was bound to become the decisive yardstick. Yet Zinovyev was his immediate superior, and Levi his personal and factional enemy. Hence he began now to steer a highly complicated course. He supported Levi in initiating new policy moves aimed at broadening the German Communists' influence on international developments, and he dropped his friends of the "Berlin Left" when they opposed these moves. But at the same time he did not cease for a moment to denounce Levi's disrespectful attitude to Comintern, his clinging to a "Luxemburgist" rather than a "Leninist" concept of the party's role, and his alleged reluctance to engage in "action"— without ever making it clear just how violent an "action" he regarded as possible in the circumstances. He thus managed to appear as the advocate both of effective support for Russia—in contrast to the sectarianism of the "Berlin Left"—and of true loyalty to Comintern and to the greater "activity" demanded by the rank and file—in contrast to Levi's scepticism. It was around this programme that he finally succeeded in rallying a majority in the leading party organs.[87]

[86] When Zinovyev disappointed them, they temporarily turned to the Russian "Workers' Opposition". Interview with Ruth Fischer.

[87] Cf. Kurt Geyer, "Zur Vorgeschichte des III Weltkongresses" in *Unser Weg*, Nr. 8/9, Aug. 1921.

The leaders of this new middle group—for such it was originally, though Radek and Comintern were quick to hail it as the new "Left" and to forget that the "Berlin Left" existed as well—came in part from the USPD like Stoecker and Koenen, in part from the old Spartacus leadership; and among the latter they included both former supporters of Levi like Thalheimer, Brandler and Pieck and seasoned critics like Froelich. Common to them all was a profound respect for Soviet and Comintern authority—and a lack of awareness of the potential conflict between the two. It was precisely this naïve ignorance of the divisions among the Bolshevik leaders that enabled these men to stick to an emotional loyalty without having to face the problems involved, and thus made them suitable for leading a "Bolshevised" Communist party: for it made them easy to manipulate for their skilful and ambiguous mentor, and at the same time representative of the mentality of their rank and file.

The first move in the new, "broad" policy jointly initiated by Levi and Radek was a "United Front offer"—a new departure in Comintern history. On January 8, 1921, the "Rote Fahne" published an Open Letter from the VKPD executive to all working class parties and trade unions in Germany, proposing cooperation in the defence of the workers' living standards, in the organisation of the workers' self-defence against the armed formations of the Right, in demanding an amnesty for left wing political prisoners, and in campaigning for the resumption of trade and diplomatic relations with Russia. The Communists, the letter explained, were not of course renouncing their more far-reaching aims, but considered joint action by all who could agree on this modest programme as the task of the moment. The proposal was contemptuously rejected by the big unions and the two socialist parties, whose leaders had for years been addressed as "traitors" by the Communists, and also by the KAPD, which in turn regarded this programme as reformist treason.[88] The latter view was also shared by a considerable section of the VKPD's own rank and file, as well as by Zinovyev and Bukharin in Moscow; but when the dispute was brought to Lenin's attention, he approved the new tactics.[89] Radek had calculated correctly.

The idea that the Communists should demand the resumption of

[88] See the chronicle for Jan. 1921 in *Kommunistische Internationale*, Nr. 16, pp. 751–3.

[89] E. H. Carr, *The Bolshevik Revolution*, III, p. 334, and *Protokoll des 3. Weltkongresses*, Hamburg, 1921, p. 511.

trade and diplomatic relations with Russia by a "bourgeois" government had an obvious propaganda value at a time of rising mass
unemployment, and a less obvious topicality at the moment when
Victor Kopp, the unofficial Soviet representative in Berlin, was about
to go home to inform Trotsky of the Reichswehr's interest in secret
Russo-German collaboration.[90] Radek was probably and Levi possibly
aware of this development; they certainly knew Lenin's speech to the
eighth Soviet congress with its statements that "Germany is naturally
pushed into alliance with Russia" and that

> "our existence depends, first, on the existence of a radical split in the
> camp of the imperialist powers, and secondly, on the fact that the
> victory of the Entente and the Versailles peace have thrown the vast
> majority of the German nation into a position where it cannot live
> . . . The German bourgeois government madly hates the Bolsheviks,
> but the interests of the international situation are pushing it towards
> peace with Soviet Russia against its own will." [91]

Hence when at the end of January the announcement by the Paris
conference of the total reparations sum to be exacted from Germany
caused a new crisis in German relations with the Entente, Levi was all
set to launch the slogan "Alliance with Soviet Russia" in a speech to
the Reichstag. He was careful to explain that he did not expect the
German capitalists to conclude that alliance, but he did not say that the
proletarian revolution would have to win first. His point was to
describe the Russian alliance as the only way to save the German
nation, and thus to use its propaganda to rally round the Communists
broad masses not only of workers but even of petty-bourgeois elements
until their pressure grew strong enough to force a change of foreign
policy and possibly of government; and he did not shy from remind-
ing the Reichstag deputies of the Russo-German feelers which had
been going on during the Soviet offensive in Poland.[92]

Whether this move, too, was concerted with Radek or not, Levi
could be sure that it would be backed in Moscow; in fact, the alliance
slogan was never criticised by Comintern and actively used under its
guidance after Levi's fall. By attacking it, the "Berlin Left" sharply
separated itself from Levi's other critics and from Comintern policy.

[90] Carr, *l.c.*, p. 361.
[91] Quoted from Lenin, *Sochinenya*, XXVI, pp. 14–15 in Carr, *l.c.*, pp. 330–1.
[92] *Rote Fahne*, Nr. 55, 3.II.21.

None the less, Radek may well have been content that his departure for Russia at this moment saved him from the need to intervene against them; for they had been making the running in attacking Levi in the party press for his alleged "inactivity",[93] and their new campaign greatly contributed to shake his authority and to spread the sense of inner-party crisis.[94]

Levi's Fall

The final conflict between Levi and Comintern arose over the split in the Italian Socialist party, provoked by the Comintern delegates to its Livorno congress, Rakosi and Kabakchiev. The Italian Socialists had formed part of the wartime Zimmerwald movement and had become the first mass party to join Comintern, even before the Second World Congress; hence they had done so without a split, carrying their reformist minority around Turati with them. At the Second World Congress Serrati, their leader, had been told that the 21 conditions would nevertheless apply also to them; and he had promised to fulfil them and expel the Turatians, asking only that he must remain free to decide the time and manner of the split.

But when Serrati returned from Moscow, he found that the factory occupation into which a great metal-workers' strike had developed had been broken off without substantial results, having perished from sheer political aimlessness; and while Comintern concluded that this was due to "reformist treason", making the expulsion of the "guilty" all the more urgent, Serrati observed that revolutionary hopes had receded and feared that the workers would be further discouraged by a split. Moreover, Turati had not, like the German right wing socialists, formed part of a government that shot at revolutionary workers, and was immensely respected as the intellectual founder of the party even by the non-reformist majority; and there was just no urgent and obvious reason why the party should be split.

As Serrati turned a deaf ear to the stream of letters and appeals from Moscow urging him to fulfil his pledge,[95] Comintern had come to rely increasingly on a left wing minority of his party, whose leader Bordiga

[93] See Friesland in *Rote Fahne*, Nr. 39, 25.I.21, and "Zur Kritik der Partei" in Nr. 57, 4.II.21. Friesland was then associated with Ruth Fischer and Maslow in Berlin.

[94] *Rote Fahne*, Nr. 75, 15.II.21; Ruth Fischer's article "Die Rettung der deutschen Nation" in Nr. 69, 11.II.21, and Friesland's "Zur Pariser Konferenz" in Nr. 71, 12.II.21.

[95] *Documents* ed. Degras, pp. 188, 192, 199 sqq.

was so "left" that he favoured the boycott of parliamentary elections; and when the Livorno congress opened on January 15, the ECCI delegates arrived with instructions to force a split on the basis of the 21 conditions—if possible, with Serrati, if necessary against him. After five days, they split against him, carrying about one-third of the votes which represented less than 60,000 members.[96]

Levi, who had come as fraternal delegate from the VKPD, was shocked by the proceedings. He kept silent at the congress, but in an editorial for his own party paper he criticised the action of the Comintern delegates.[97] Officially he argued on the basis of the 21 conditions, claiming only that to break with the majority of a great workers' party in order to get rid of a minority of reformists was the wrong manner of enforcing them: a patient struggle to convince the majority first would have been needed rather than a hurried mechanical split. But the inner logic of this argument was plainly directed against the 21 conditions themselves—he had, after all, never believed in this method, precisely because "mechanical splitting" was its very essence. He had tried to make the best of them in Germany when the USPD workers were moving to the Left, but to continue splitting mass parties now that the revolutionary wave was receding seemed to him obvious folly. But this was a basically non-Bolshevik view: it meant that Levi was moving to the conclusion that the principle of separating out a small, revolutionary core even in non-revolutionary times, on which the Bolshevik tradition was founded, was not applicable to the revolutionary minorities in the mass organisations of Western and Central Europe.

It was the tactical weakness of Levi's position that he did not wish to proclaim this conclusion at that stage. He hoped that Lenin might be persuaded of its truth, but felt sure that Zinovyev and his Comintern apparatus could not be made to see it unless the Bolshevik Central Committee saw it first, and for that time was needed.[98] Hence Levi tried to evade a debate on fundamentals at this moment; but Radek had no difficulty in divining the drift of his thought from his cautious public criticism. He counter-attacked not only with three articles

[96] *Ibid.*, pp. 208–9.

[97] *Rote Fahne*, Nr. 17, 23.I.21.

[98] In a letter to Radek, Levi wrote: "The correction of the (Comintern) executive's mistakes will take place. It can only take place from Russia. Concrete proposals or criticism on our part at this moment would not change the situation, but only disturb our relations with the executive. I have reasons for this opinion." *Rote Fahne*, Nr. 53, 2.II.21.

defending the Italian split in the party paper,[99] but with a blunt threat in a meeting of the party executive ("Before you attack us, we shall act first and shall draw the sword against you"), which caused Levi to put the formal question whether the ECCI or its representative in Germany regarded his removal as joint chairman of the party as necessary or desirable, and to leave the meeting. The answer, by then, was clearly yes; in a letter written on the following day, Radek did not reply directly and even apologised for the form of his attack, but charged Levi with trying systematically to undermine the ECCI's authority.[100]

The next meeting of the party executive, on February 1st, was faced with two resolutions on the Italian split—Levi's cautiously critical, Radek's unreservedly supporting the ECCI. In a letter addressed to this meeting, Radek insisted on a clear decision: "Better that the party chairman should be placed in the minority within the executive for once, than that the executive should, from a desire to back him up, not only adopt a centrist policy but even try to hide this fact from the party." [101] To avoid defeat on an "exotic" issue Levi withdrew his resolution, and Radek's draft was adopted with some amendments which blunted its endorsement of ECCI's action by recommending further negotiations with the Serratians so as not to lose their honest revolutionary workers.[102]

But it was now obvious that the decisive clash was at hand. The same meeting of the executive adopted a proposal to improve the working of ECCI which reflected Levi's concern that the Russian party should see the problems of other movements through the eyes of responsible Russians and not only of Hungarian, Bulgarian or Polish exiles.[103] A week later Levi reviewed all his disputes with Comintern at a meeting of Berlin party workers. On two issues, he still had the backing of a united party executive—the old quarrel about the KAP, and the difficulties caused to Communist trade union work by the tendency of Profintern to welcome syndicalist splinter unions.[104] But he also repeated his arguments against the Italian split, and he replied for the first time publicly to Comintern's doctrine of the revolutionary offen-

[99] "P.B." in *Rote Fahne*, Nr. 41–3 of 26. and 27.I.21.

[100] Radek's threat and his subsequent letter are quoted in Levi's reply which also repeated the question whether Comintern wished to remove him. The reply is the letter referred to in note 98 above.

[101] Radek, *Soll die VKPD*, pp. 45–53.

[102] *Rote Fahne*, Nr. 53, 2.II.21.

[103] *Ibid.*   [104] *Ibid.*, Nr. 59, 5.II.21.

sive, which had just been systematically expounded in an article by Bukharin:[105] it was wrong to think of introducing the Soviet system in other countries "at the point of the bayonet"—to be stable, Soviet power required a basis in the revolutionary will of the proletariat in each country.[106]

This speech, and the news that Serrati had come to Berlin and talked with Levi, decided Radek's supporters in the party executive to bring matters to a head.[107] Led by Thalheimer and Stoecker, they submitted a "tightened up" resolution of unconditional support for the ECCI's Italian policy to the next meeting of the party's "Zentralausschuss" (Central Committee—at that time a periodic conference of the executive with representatives of all districts) which met on February 22. It went beyond the executive's last compromise text in explicitly endorsing all the actions of the ECCI delegates in Livorno and demanding an "uncompromising struggle" against Serrati;[108] Levi could not possibly accept it, yet had no clear basis for opposing it since he was committed to the earlier evasive formula.

But all evasion was swept away when Rakosi, accidentally passing through Berlin, appeared at the meeting and defended his Livorno conduct on the ground that "if regard for the clarity of the Communist party makes such splits imperative, they have to be carried out, if necessary ten times, whether in Italy, France or Germany".[109] To this, Levi opposed his warning that the method of forming small but pure parties by recurrent splits, which might have had its value in the Russian pre-war underground movement, would prove fatal if applied to the mass organisations which the West European workers regarded as indispensable to their action. Yet, in the end, unconditional support for the ECCI's action in Italy obtained 28 votes against 23:[110] in a straight test of authority and confidence, a majority of the responsible officials of the VKPD preferred to trust the judgment of ECCI rather than that of their own elected leaders.

After this, the two chairmen of the party, Levi and Daeumig, as well

[105] Cf. note 85 above.

[106] *Rote Fahne*, Nr. 67 of 10.II.21. Also Levi's two articles in Nr. 59 and 60 of 5.II.21.

[107] Radek, "Die Krise in der VKPD", *Die Internationale*, III, 3, 1.IV.21, p. 75.

[108] *Rote Fahne*, Nr. 97, 27.II.21.

[109] This statement of Rakosi's is not quoted from unpublished minutes, but from the official report in *Rote Fahne*, Nr. 95, 26.II.21, where Rakosi appears under the pseudonym Marboczi. Cf. also his letter in *Rote Fahne*, Nr. 99, 1.III.21.

[110] *Ibid.*, Nr. 97, 27.II.21.

as Klara Zetkin and two other members of the executive—altogether 5 of its 14 members, later followed by a sixth, Kurt Geyer, who was then in Moscow—resigned their offices, stating in a joint declaration that they could not share responsibility for "the attempt to create purer and more solid Communist parties by the mechanical process of splitting" which was bound to destroy the parties' mass influence.[111] They were replaced by supporters of the majority; Brandler and Stoecker became the new joint chairmen, and the newly elected members of the executive included Ernst Meyer and Froelich.[112] In a counter-declaration to that of the resigning leaders, the new majority asserted that it had merely voted for loyal cooperation with the ECCI; it saw no issue of principle in the dispute and no need for new splits in the German party.[113]

But the differences of principle which the victorious middle group could not see were obvious both to Levi and to the Comintern leaders. A few days later, Levi told a meeting of Berlin party activists that he and his friends had protested against the Italian split "because we know that this split is based on a theoretical concept which Lenin vigorously defended as far back as 1903, 1904 and 1905, and which Rosa Luxemburg fought as vigorously at the time".[114] Zinovyev, reporting to the Russian party congress in mid-March, gave it as his and Radek's joint opinion that Levi had been "predestined" for veering off to the Right, and that an ideological struggle against his opportunist tendency could no longer be postponed.[115] And in an article for the theoretical journal of the VKPD, Radek stated that it was wrong for the new German party executive to try and smooth over the conflict. Levi and his group had been unable "to pass from the forced defensive of 1919 to the increasing offensive made possible by the radicalisation of masses of USPD workers in 1920"; now he was inventing the bogey of "mechanical splits" because ECCI had been attacking his own inactivity which threatened the future of the party. The issues in dispute, Radek continued, "if they may be clarified by discussions, can be conclusively settled only by actions"; that was the only way to liquidate Levi's "theory of inactivity". "It is easier to accept 21 Communist theses than to lead the masses one step forward in practical struggle. The VKPD has not yet made this first practical

[111] *Rote Fahne*, Nr. 98, 28.II.21.
[112] *Ibid.*, Nr. 99, 1.III.21.   [113] *Ibid.*
[114] *Ibid.*, Nr. 101, 2.III.21.
[115] *Kommunistische Internationale*, Nr. 16, pp. 555 sqq.

step . . . That is the surest proof of the party's crisis: it is not fighting yet." [116]

Thus the basic issue, which Levi had seen as the choice between the formation of revolutionary parties by mechanical splitting from without, or organic growth based on their own experience, was defined from the other side as turning on Comintern's right to prod its affiliated parties into offensive action according to its own judgment. Radek's article was dated March 15. A few days later, the new leadership of the VKPD was indeed engaged in an "offensive" struggle, prompted by the advice of a new representative of Comintern. The "March Action" had begun.

The March Action

With the resignation of Levi and his supporters from the party executive, the principal obstacle to effective Comintern control of the policy of the VKPD had disappeared. Though the party's heterogeneous composition and factional groupings showed how far it was still removed from the Bolshevik ideal of a truly "centralised" or "monolithic" party, we must not forget that even the Russian Communist Party, for all its ideology of centralism and all its responsibilities of dictatorial power, was in March 1921 only just about to adopt a formal ban on the formation of factions: up to then, Bolshevik centralism had chiefly depended on the growth of Lenin's personal authority, and on the inherent needs of the dictatorship. In the same way, the decisive step in the Bolshevisation of the German party, too, was the establishment of an uncontested authority—the authority of the Russian state party as embodied in the directives of Comintern. With the first overthrow of an indigenous leadership under Comintern pressure, that step had manifestly been taken.

We know from Radek's article that Comintern now felt free to reconstruct the German party by an ideological struggle against the "Luxemburgist" traditions of the "right wing", and by pushing it into the kind of action which its former leaders had resisted. In practice, the task fell to a new Comintern representative sent to Germany at the end of February or the beginning of March—Bela Kun. Kun's mission had not been discussed in any plenary session of ECCI;[117] on the eve of his departure he had been promoted to membership of its Little Bureau,[118]

[116] Radek, "Die Krise in der VKPD", *Die Internationale*, III, 3, 1.IV.21, pp. 71–9.
[117] Interview Kurt Geyer (who represented VKPD in ECCI at the time).
[118] *Rote Fahne*, Nr. 102, 2.III.21.

normally reserved to permanent residents of Moscow, and we do not know whether the instructions he received in this small circle went beyond Radek's ambiguities in defining the kind of action that was expected. But his very selection was a programme, for ever since the defeat of the Hungarian Soviet Republic he had headed, he had been notorious both for the "left" extremism of his views and for the unscrupulousness of his methods in the factional struggles among the Hungarian exiles.

When Kun arrived with his two assistants, his countryman Pogamy and the Pole Guralski, the reparations issue was about to reach a new crisis. Negotiations between the Reich and the allied powers on the Paris demands had dragged on in London for weeks; when Germany finally refused to accept the figure, the Entente decided on March 8 to impose military and economic sanctions—an extension of the occupied zone in the Rhineland and the creation of a customs line between it and the rest of Germany. Conflict was also brewing over the allied demand that the German "Einwohnerwehren" (local citizen's guards) were to be disarmed; as these were important chiefly as a party force of the Right, the middle-of-the-road Reich government, headed by Fehrenbach of the Centre party, was willing to comply, but the right wing Bavarian government of von Kahr refused to disarm its "Orgesch". Finally, the Upper Silesian plebiscite was due on March 20, and seemed pregnant with armed conflict between Germany and Poland.

But the first days of March were also a time of acute crisis in Russia. Following a strike wave in Petrograd and food riots in Moscow, the Soviet government on March 6 officially admitted the mutiny of the Kronstadt sailors, "explaining" it by counter-revolutionary machinations incited from abroad. To Kun and the German Communist leaders advised by him, this was proof for the Comintern thesis that a new bout of allied intervention against the Soviets, to be carried out by Poland and the other border states, was closely impending. In fact, they saw the Kronstadt rising and the London ultimatum as part of a single Entente plot, aimed both at crushing the Russian revolution and at isolating Germany as a helpless object of exploitation.[119]

It followed from this analysis that the campaign for an alliance with Soviet Russia had to be resumed with a new urgency in order to save both the German nation and the Russian revolution; even Levi was now allowed to write a signed article demanding concentration on this

[119] *Rote Fahne*, Nr. 114, 9.III.21.

point.[120] But Kun and the party executive insisted now on combining this slogan with a demand for the overthrow of the Fehrenbach government,[121] which had shelved all thought of regular diplomatic relations with the Soviets ever since the Russian retreat from Warsaw. Any alternative government, they argued, whether more to the Right or to the Left, would bring about a sharpening of domestic conflicts and thus improve the Communists' chances.[122] Moreover, overthrowing the government seemed a more tangible objective for mass action than the Russian alliance by itself.

But the masses showed little inclination to go into action for either slogan: after all, neither the new hunger blockade prophesied by the Communists as a result of allied sanctions, nor the new war of intervention, had so far become a fact. Leading members of the party executive have later described the workers' mood in those critical weeks as "leaden lethargy",[123] and talked of a "wall of passivity".[124] But Kun was not discouraged; in the next few days he unveiled both to the new leaders of the party and to Klara Zetkin and Levi, who were still its chief spokesmen in the Reichstag, his project for an action which the VKPD should start on its own initiative, without waiting for a spontaneous mass movement.[125] Though Zetkin and Levi were horrified, their successors were quickly won over, and on March 17 they developed the same ideas to a full session of the broader Central Committee with the district secretaries.[126]

The international crisis, they argued, threatened the German workers with a new, intolerable worsening of their living conditions. A Communist mass party could not wait "passively" for mass resistance to this threat; its duty was to set the example of such resistance by its own independent action, thus further sharpening the crisis and "forcing the destiny of the revolution and its own". It was able to do this because its influence had grown so strong that it could count on two or three million workers outside the party to join its half million members

[120] *Ibid.*, Nr. 115, 10.III.21.

[121] See the appeal by the party executive in the same issue.

[122] Paul Froelich, "Offensive" in *Die Internationale*, III, 3, p. 67, and Levi, *Unser Weg—Wider den Putschismus*, second edition, Berlin, 1921, pp. 6–11.

[123] Paul Froelich in the article quoted in the previous note.

[124] A. Thalheimer, "Die internationale und innere Lage ..." in *Taktik und Organisation der revolutionaeren Offensive*, Leipzig-Berlin, 1921, p. 15.

[125] Paul Levi, *Was ist das Verbrechen*, Berlin, 1921, p. 15.

[126] Levi in *Unser Weg—Wider den Putschismus*, Berlin, 1921, which quotes the minutes on pp. 30–2.

even in offensive action. The immediate goal was not the seizure of power, but the overthrow of the weak government which would come tumbling down if given a strong push. The slogans were to combine the attack on the government with the demands for an alliance with Russia and for better wages. The means envisaged were mass strikes, to be developed into armed struggle if police, Reichswehr or right wing organisations attacked the striking workers; if necessary, such attacks were to be provoked in order to broaden the mass movement. The action was to begin as soon as possible after the Easter holidays (March 27/8).

But even while the meeting of March 17 was in progress, news arrived which seriously changed the plan. The Social-democratic chief administrator of the Prussian province of Saxony, Hoersing, had announced that some parts of the Central German industrial region, notably the Mansfeld area, were to be occupied by police, allegedly because of the growing number of industrial thefts, wildcat strikes and acts of violence there. The Communists could have no doubt that his real purpose was to disarm their organisations;[127] for the province of Halle, which included the designated areas, was not only a Communist political stronghold, but the centre of their strongest military cadres. The left wing of the USPD had long maintained a secret military organisation, centrally led by Daeumig; and after the destruction of the Ruhr units in the Kapp days, its other main force in Central Germany had been absorbed by the VKPD and was now, after Daeumig's resignation, in process of being reorganised by the old Communist Eberlein.[128]

Hoersing's move thus confronted the Communist leaders with the choice of either quietly suffering the disarming of their strongest military cadres at the very time when they were preparing for offensive action, or accepting combat at a time and place and on an issue chosen by their opponents. Though they regarded Hoersing's announcement as a deliberate provocation, they felt unable to evade it. The delegates of the Halle district were instructed to proclaim a general strike as soon as the police occupied any factories or mines, and to prepare for stepping up resistance to the point of armed struggle. The plan of waiting until after Easter and of launching the movement in response

[127] *Die Maerzkaempfe 1921* (Marx-Engels-Lenin-Stalin Institute), Berlin, 1956. This account suppresses every mention of the role of the ECCI and Bela Kun, but gives documents on Hoersing's measures which appear authentic.
[128] Hugo Eberlein, "M.P.", *Rote Fahne*, Nr. 593 and 595, 28./29.XII.21.

to the international crisis had thus been abandoned in favour of immediate local resistance to police measures for the disarming of the
Central German Communists; yet the general idea that a nation-wide
"offensive" mass movement could be created by the party at will,
however accidental the occasion, remained and determined the strategy
adopted.[129]

The first police units—two separate detachments of just over 500
men each—moved into two selected areas on Saturday, March 19.[130]
But already on the 18th the "Rote Fahne" carried an appeal calling on
all workers to take up arms: "Every worker defies the law and gets
himself a weapon where he finds it!" The appeal was not specially
addressed to Central Germany and was *not* based on Hoersing's
announcement—it had, in fact, been drafted by Kun before that was
known—but on the refusal of the Bavarian government to disarm the
Orgesch.[131] It had not been discussed by the party executive, let alone
by the broader meeting of the previous day; Kun had simply persuaded
the party chairman, Brandler, to have it printed.[132] When the issue
was confiscated, it was reprinted on the next day's front page; and it
was followed by a series of unsigned calls to arms for several days
running before there had been any clash in Central Germany, and
before the party executive had even officially called for a general
strike.[133]

Events in Central Germany developed with similar absurdity. Contrary to Communist expectation, the police at first occupied no factories or mines, and quietly waited for things to happen. The Mansfeld
party organisation nevertheless threatened a general strike unless the
police was withdrawn, and the strike began on Monday the 21st, but
only in the occupied area—even the party's district executive at Halle
still felt unable to call for mass action. Instead, military preparations
were frantically discussed, at the insistence of the Comintern delegates,
jointly with the KAPD. On the 22nd, Eberlein told the Halle leaders
that events which would act as a signal for a nation-wide movement
must be produced at all cost in Central Germany, and discussed the
need for provoking the police and inciting the workers by feigned

[129] Froelich's article quoted in notes 122 and 123 above.
[130] *Rote Fahne*, Nr. 133, 20.III.21; *Die Maerzkaempfe 1921*, pp. 23, 169–72.
[131] *Rote Fahne*, Nr. 129, 18.III; 131, 19.III.21.
[132] Bernhard Duewell, "Disziplin und Grundaetze" in Levi's periodical *Sowjet*,
III, 1, 1.V.21; interview Heinrich Brandler.
[133] *Rote Fahne*, Nr. 133, 134 of 20./21.III.21.

attacks on their institutions and leaders. On that same day, however, Max Hoelz, a revolutionary guerilla leader then working with KAPD, had in mass meetings in the Mansfeld area called on the workers to arm themselves; that night, workers at Eisleben took over an arms dump, and on Wednesday the 23rd, fighting started throughout the occupied district. On the news of this, the workers of the Leuna chemical works declared a strike and occupied the grounds; the Halle district committee proclaimed a general strike from the following day; and on the 24th, the Thursday before Easter, the VKPD executive issued its formal appeal for a nation-wide general strike.[134]

It turned out a complete fiasco. Sporadic local fighting by Communist military units in Central Germany continued for about a week, against reinforced police and in one or two cases against Reichswehr; on the whole, the latter confined itself to isolating the danger zone without entering it. Halle saw no fighting—the Communist units there felt so isolated that they preferred to march to the Mansfeld area and join in the clashes there. Leuna surrendered on the morning of the 29th after some artillery shells had been fired at it, but the workers' fighting organisation had disintegrated before.[135] There was some local shooting also in Hamburg and in two small Rhineland towns.

As for the strike, far from involving "two or three million workers" it remained almost entirely confined to Communist party members, many of whom lost their jobs; only in parts of Central Germany and of the Ruhr was there a broader participation for a few days.[136] In many cases, unemployed Communists tried to "persuade" employed workers by force to come out, and were chased away by them with bloody noses.[137] On April 1st, the party executive at last called off the movement, admitting its defeat but claiming proudly that it had proved its serious will and ability to fight.[138]

In asking why the German Communists were pushed into this adventure, we may safely discard the view that the Soviet leaders embarked on this desperate expedient in a last attempt to avoid the

---

[134] Froelich's "Die Maerzaktion" in *Taktik und Organisation der revolutionaeren Offensive*, Berlin-Leipzig, 1921 for the contemporary official communist record; for the disclosures of local communist military leaders see *Die Blutschuld der Kommunisten* (Vorwaerts and Paul Singer, Berlin, 1921).

[135] *Die Maerzkaempfe 1921*, pp. 27–32, 82.

[136] *Protokoll des 3 Weltkongresses*, Hamburg, 1921, pp. 249–51.

[137] Levi, *Unser Weg—Wider den Putschismus*, p. 40, and *Was ist das Verbrechen?*, p. 23.

[138] *Rote Fahne*, Nr. 159, 4.IV.21.

"retreat" of the New Economic Policy. When Kun left Moscow, Lenin was already engaged in pushing the new policy through the Central Committee; and on March 12, five days before the "March Action" was decided on, the "Rote Fahne" reported Lenin's opening speech to the Tenth Congress of the Bolshevik party to the effect that "we must in no case base our calculations on a quick victory of World Revolution".[139] Kun can thus have been under no illusions that, in precipitating a revolutionary adventure in Germany at that moment, he was carrying out Lenin's will.

But neither can the responsibility be attributed to Kun alone. If Zinovyev did not positively instruct him to engineer an armed rising —which he may not have dared without the approval of the Russian Politbureau—the instructions must have been so vague and the powers so broad that, given Kun's views and character, the outcome was foreseeable. It follows that not only Kun, but Zinovyev and the "Little Bureau" of Comintern wanted this kind of action. A success in overthrowing the German government, even if its successor was more to the Right, might have speeded up the resumption of diplomatic relations with Russia; and if this result was brought about by Comintern action, would it not have come as a welcome proof of Comintern's continued importance in the new period of co-existence and manœuvre?

While the role played by such calculations in the policy of Comintern must remain speculative, another motive is clearly documented: the desire to purge the German movement of its "opportunist" elements, to speed up its further Bolshevisation by pushing it into "action". Apart from Radek's article of March 15,[140] this is confirmed by the contribution of another Comintern official, under the pseudonym Franz Richter, to a pamphlet in defence of the March Action compiled immediately afterwards by the German party executive: he claimed that the action's "most important result for the labour movement was that the opportunist trend was forced to reveal itself, and that thereby the crisis of the party turned the corner from the process of decay to the process of purification".[141]

That was indeed the only one of the action's objectives which was actually achieved. The Reich government was not overthrown. The destruction of the Communist military cadres in Central Germany was

[139] *Ibid.*, Nr. 119, 12.III.21. [140] Cf. note 116 above.
[141] Franz Richter, "Organisatorisches zur Maerzaktion" in *Taktik und Organisation der revolutionaeren Offensive*, Berlin-Leipzig, 1921.

not prevented, but actually facilitated by their improvised rising. Apart from the hundreds who lost their lives and the larger number who landed in gaol, the Communist party as a whole was gravely weakened. A deep gulf had been created between it and the non-Communist workers; its trade union influence was all but destroyed; its membership was reduced to less than half in the prolonged crisis that followed. But the crisis did largely purge the party of its "right wing", i.e. of those elements, headed by Levi, who represented what was left in it of Rosa Luxemburg's tradition.

The "Luxemburgists" leave

The outward occasion for the breach was Levi's publication of a pamphlet—"Our Road: Against Putschism" [142]—which not only condemned the "March Action" and the "theory of the offensive" but disclosed, without giving names, the outline of its secret history and the role played by the plenipotentiary of Comintern, and went on to criticise the whole working of ECCI and its delegates abroad. The pamphlet came out on April 12; on the 15th, Levi was expelled by the party executive as a "renegade and slanderer";[143] on the 16th, Zetkin, Daeumig and other former leading party officials vouched publicly for the facts and quotations published by Levi.[144] The Russians then intervened to prevent the wholesale expulsion of this group, and after the policy change of Comintern's Third Congress succeeded in retaining Zetkin and a few of the others; but Levi himself could no longer be brought back into the fold.[145] Formally, his unforgivable crime was that he had made a public, frontal attack on the authority of Comintern and would not withdraw it; in fact, his refusal to compromise on this point was a consequence of his realisation of the unbridgeable difference between his own, "Luxemburgist" concept of the revolutionary party and the Bolshevik one—a difference far transcending the particular issue of the March Action.

In Levi's and Radek's pamphlets of this period,[146] that difference found its final and indeed classical formulation. Its most obvious aspect

[142] *Unser Weg—Wider den Putschismus.*

[143] *Rote Fahne*, Nr. 169, 16.IV.21.   [144] *Ibid.*, Nr. 171, 17.IV.21.

[145] Zetkin: *Erinnerungen an Lenin*, Berlin-Wien, 1929, pp. 32–5, 40–1.

[146] One month after *Unser Weg—Wider den Putschismus* Levi published *Was ist das Verbrechen? Die Maerzaktion oder die Kritik daran.* This is the text of his address to the May meeting of the Central Committee which had to hear his appeal against his expulsion. Radek's position is summed up in *Soll die VKPD eine Massenpartei der revolutionaeren Aktion oder eine zentristische Partei des Wartens sein?*

concerned the relation between Comintern and its affiliated parties. Levi argued that actions like that precipitated by Kun—whether or not based on actual instructions from the ECCI—were only made possible by Comintern's claim for absolute authority, combined with its failure to offer genuine political guidance based on a serious study of international developments. As a substitute for such guidance, he charged, Comintern had concentrated on purging its affiliated mass parties from alleged "Menshevik" tendencies without regard to the actual political situation, and conferred vast powers over these parties on its delegates; and as the Russian Bolsheviks would not spare their own best men from urgent domestic tasks, these powers had come to be exercised by various would-be statesmen eager to demonstrate their revolutionary prowess, often ignorant of conditions in their assigned territory, and yet entitled to report to ECCI over the heads of the homegrown leadership and liable to find greater credence there. It would be better if these eager beavers were assigned, say, Soviet Turkestan as their exercise ground;[147] as it was, ECCI was having the effect of "a Cheka projected beyond the Soviet frontiers".[148]

But Levi was aware that the validity of this criticism depended on one's view of the desirable structure of the Communist parties themselves. If only a centralised *élite* party on the model of the pre-war Bolsheviks could be truly revolutionary, the splitting tactics practised by the ECCI's delegates might eventually bring about that result. Yet Comintern itself claimed that it wanted not sects, but revolutionary mass parties; and Levi argued that in countries with the traditions of a broad, democratic labour movement, mass parties could only survive if they were not sealed off from the state of mind of the bulk of the working class, but were open to its influences as well as influencing it.[149] But such a mass party could no more be ordered into action than the class of which it formed a part: the conscious vanguard could explain the situation to the masses and show them a way forward by its propaganda, but, in the words of Rosa Luxemburg, it must leave to history the moment when a revolutionary mass movement would actually arise.[150] If it tried instead to give ultimative orders to the masses, the inevitable outcome in European conditions was self-isolation and disaster.

Even beyond this problem of the relation of vanguard and masses,

[147] *Unser Weg—Wider den Putschismus*, p. 54. [148] *Ibid.*, p. 56.
[149] *Was ist das Verbrechen?* pp. 20–1; *Unser Weg*, pp. 37–8.
[150] The quotation from Rosa Luxemburg is in *Was ist das Verbrechen?*, p. 19.

the last and crucial aspect of the dispute concerned the future of a separate revolutionary party in a non-revolutionary situation. Levi still agreed with the Bolsheviks that such parties were both possible and necessary to prepare for the next revolutionary chance. But he foresaw that if the waiting period should be long, the split between a reformist and a revolutionary mass movement might become fixed along lines of social stratification, with the skilled workers in good bargaining positions and strong unions gravitating to the reformists, and the Communists attracting the desperate unemployed, occasionally reinforced by the lumpenproletariat. Convinced that no true proletarian revolution could be accomplished without the solid core of self-reliant, militant trade unionists, he found the ultimate ground for his rejection of separate minority action in this fear that such a policy, by attracting the most desperate strata only and repelling the solid core, would create an unbridgeable *social* gulf between the revolutionary minority and the main force of the working class.[151]

But the division of the movement along lines of social stratification which Levi was so anxious to avoid was to the Bolsheviks the very essence of the split. Ever since the war, Lenin had demanded the split precisely because he regarded reformism as the politics of a corrupt workers' aristocracy; and when the majority of European workers failed to rally to the Communist banner, Radek had the consistency to demand that the party should boldly use the revolutionary potential of the unemployed in separate actions. In an article written after Levi's resignation as party leader, he branded Levi's warnings against any community with lumpenproletarian elements as showing a failure to understand the growing importance of the unemployed masses in a period of structural crisis of capitalism, and attacked him for his unwillingness to use their revolutionary potential.[152] But Levi did not regard the unemployed workers as part of the lumpenproletariat, that collection of the products of decay from all classes, so long as they still felt and acted as workers. With the experience of the March Action behind him, he answered that the party's task was precisely to maintain the ties between employed and unemployed workers—not to push the unemployed down into the lumpenproletariat by setting them against the employed and using them for provocations.[153]

[151] *Was ist das Verbrechen?*, p. 21. See also Levi, "Die Aufgaben der Kommunisten" in his periodical *Unser Weg*, Nr. 5, 1.VII.21.

[152] Radek, "Die Krise in der VKPD", *Die Internationale*, III, 3, April 1, 1921, pp. 73-4.   [153] *Unser Weg—Wider den Putschismus*, pp. 43-7.

Now Radek still further broadened the issue by boldly attacking the belief that the German Communists had captured a substantial part of the traditional core of organised labour by their fusion with the left wing of the USPD. The overwhelming majority of the old social-democratic membership, he asserted, was still in SPD and USPD; the overwhelming majority of the VKPD members were people who had been awakened to political activity only by the shocks of war and revolution. But this formation of the VKPD chiefly from new political elements was "an advantage", for the old SPD membership had largely consisted of worker-aristocrats unfit for revolutionary struggle![154]

It is clear in retrospect that neither protagonist was yet conscious of the full implications of the position then taken by him. Radek's distrust of the traditionally organised workers as "aristocrats" and his reliance on the violent despair of strata cut off from production logically implied that he did not necessarily want a working class party at all, but a party using all available elements of social disruption for the seizure of power—in short, a modern totalitarian party. Levi's fear that a prolonged split between reformist and revolutionary mass parties would lead to a division along lines of social stratification, and his insistence that the revolutionary vanguard must not separate itself from the core of the working class in action, logically implied that if the non-revolutionary situation lasted, he would wish to return to Rosa Luxemburg's pre-war position—that of a minority within a single, united party. The separate revolutionary mass party could survive in the long run only if it became as fundamentally "classless", as capable of changing its "social basis" according to the situation, as all totalitarian parties; the working class character of the party could only be preserved in the long run if the split was abandoned. But it took time for both sides to become aware of this.

Some Conclusions

Within a few months of Levi's expulsion, a change of tactics was forced on Comintern by the Russian party, and more particularly by Lenin and Trotsky, exactly as he had expected. The Third World Congress formally condemned the "theory of the offensive" and proclaimed the new general line of keeping "closer to the masses". But it did not admit that the condemned theory had been the cause of the March Action and had been imposed by Comintern; it confirmed the

[154] *Soll die VKPD* . . . , pp. 15–17.

expulsion of Levi for having said so; and it did not even discuss the underlying differences of principle. For the future of the German Communist Party, the tactical victory of the "Right" at the Third World Congress thus proved less important than the preservation of the myth of Comintern's infallibility and the purge of the "Luxemburgists", for that purge completed what the Comintern-imposed change of leadership had begun: the first phase of the Bolshevisation of the KPD.

The question why this operation, which by then had not yet become routine, was accomplished so quickly and with such comparative ease may be answered on different levels. On the personal level, Levi's weaknesses no doubt helped the work of his opponents. His personal isolation and lack of the popular touch made him an easy target for denigrating attack; his tendency to retire when hurt robbed the influence of continuity which his superior insight could have commanded; his lack of control over his own moral and political indignation caused him to challenge Comintern over the Italian issue, which few members of his party could be expected to understand, and though he knew it would have been wiser to postpone the struggle until after the Russian party congress. Clearly, a man of this temper was no match for an unscrupulous manipulator of Radek's gifts, who was always ready to fight for particular views in which he did not believe provided this was likely to strengthen his tactical position on the major issue.

On the level of organisational techniques, we have noted the early use by Comintern of methods which have since become commonplace: the deliberate mixing of different elements to create a less homogeneous and more pliable leadership; the encouragement of the formation of "wings" which Comintern could then play against each other; the incorporation in party documents of general key phrases which could later be applied as yardsticks for measuring the performance of the leaders; the gradual building up of inner-party legends about recalcitrant leaders in order to discredit them, first by whispering, then publicly through the mouth of opponents, finally by open use of Comintern's authority; the interference of Comintern's delegates with their right to obtain information and give "advice" at all levels, to write in the party's press against its leaders and to exert massive pressure behind the scenes.

But neither the personal factors nor Comintern's "tricks of the trade" compare in importance with the major political causes of its easy victory. The first of these is the unique authority conferred on Comintern by the victorious consolidation of Soviet Russia, and the contrasting failure of all non-Bolshevik revolutionary movements. To those European Socialists who wanted a proletarian revolution, Russia was by 1920 the only successful model, and the Bolsheviks had not been slow to assume the role of international leaders and teachers. The USPD had not been split over a concrete issue of German politics, but over the 21 conditions, i.e. over the principle of formal obedience to the dictates of Comintern; hence from the moment of fusion, the authority of Comintern meant more to the great majority of the members of the united party than that of any of their own leaders. The decisive transfer of authority had happened then—what followed was merely the working out of its implications.

Another major political cause may be found in the dilemma of a revolutionary mass party in a non-revolutionary situation. The very fact of the split attracts to such a party not only theoretical believers in the need for revolution, but all those who, be it for reasons of their desperate social situation or of their personal temperament, want revolutionary action here and now; hence the natural drift from below in any Communist party is always to the "Left", and "right turns" imposed from above always meet much greater resistance than "left turns". Thus in a situation when responsible leaders could not gratify the desire of the rank and file for revolutionary action, Comintern had only to ride this current in order to break up the cohesion of the leadership and defeat its most independent-minded elements. More fundamentally, we have seen above that in a prolonged non-revolutionary situation, insistence on avoiding separate minority actions must logically lead to the return to a single, united party: hence all the momentum of the split, all the material and emotional interests vested in the existence of a separate revolutionary party were on the side of Comintern.

But behind those two proximate political causes we may discern an ultimately decisive historic fact. The transfer of authority to Comintern was based on the failure of all non-Bolshevik revolutionary movements in Europe. The leftward drift of the Communist rank and file sprang from the impossibility of maintaining in the long run a separate revolutionary party with a "Luxemburgist" concept of its role. But both circumstances really expressed the fact—more obvious today than at the time—that the basic expectation of Rosa Luxemburg, and of the non-Bolshevik revolutionary Marxists generally, had been disproved by history: the expectation that the working class of industrially advanced Europe would be increasingly revolutionised by its own experience. It is thus no accident that all the European revolutionary Marxist groups of the pre-1914 era, inasmuch as they clung to this assumption and did not submit to the ideological transformation imposed by Comintern, have ended as insignificant sects outside or as equally uninfluential groups inside the social-democratic parties. In the last analysis, the heirs of Rosa Luxemburg were defeated by the "Bolshevisers" because their own vision of the proletarian revolution had no future.

Why, then, were the efforts of Comintern to create "revolutionary" mass parties and subject them to Bolshevik discipline not defeated just as effectively by the failure of the European workers to become revolutionary? It is true that none of these parties has ever seized power by its own efforts in an advanced industrial country. But it is equally obvious that many of them have proved viable in a different sense—that they have preserved a mass following while maintaining a "revolutionary" attitude of disloyalty towards the state and society in which they operate. The explanation of this relative success seems to be that these parties have, in the manner anticipated by Radek, accepted the consequences of the split and of their new, "Bolshevik" methods of organisation and action: they have renounced the attempt to remain authentic workers' parties bound to specific class interests, and have increasingly become classless parties of the uprooted and disaffected, finding a focus of faith and loyalty in the power of the Soviet state far more than in the mission of the proletariat. The growth of free industrial societies has nowhere driven the working class to revolution; but it tends to uproot again and again particular sections of all classes, including the workers, from their productive functions and to deprive them temporarily of material and psychological security. The Communists, like all totalitarian parties, are enabled by their centralist form of organisation to rely on such varying groups as the occasion offers, while their link with a great power allows them to show a beacon of hope to those who can no longer help themselves by democratic means.

Yet while these present-day Communist parties are the final outcome of the process of Bolshevisation of which we have described the beginning, they are almost as far removed from the original Bolshevik hopes of World Revolution as from the concepts of the non-Bolshevik revolutionary Marxists. Significantly, Lenin's role in the opening stage of this process appears from our account to have been rather less prominent than that of the *apparachiki* of Comintern, and at times even downright ambivalent. True, it was Lenin himself who first staked the claim of Bolshevism to be a model for proletarian revolution everywhere, and who sought to embody it in the 21 conditions. But he still genuinely believed that he was dealing with a revolution of the working class, just as he maintained this belief inside Russia even while he was in fact laying the foundations of a totalitarian party régime of a new type; and whenever he came up against the unforeseen consequences of his own actions—consequences in obvious contradiction with his view of himself as leader of a working class movement—he hesitated in the international field just as he often did at home. It was not Lenin himself, for all his traditional differences with Rosa Luxemburg's school, who conceived the idea of "purging" her pupils from the German Communist party by driving the party into an irresponsible adventure; nor did he welcome this result when it was achieved, as his conversations with Klara Zetkin and his subsequent letter to the Jena congress of the KPD show beyond possible doubt. Just as in Russian domestic affairs he was less willing to accept the totalitarian logic of the one-party state than Stalin was to be, so in international affairs he was less willing to accept the logic of the permanent split and of the subordination of the Communist parties to Moscow than were Zinovyev and Radek. If Lenin could have foreseen the final outcome of the process which we have designated as the Bolshevisation of the Communist parties, he might well have sincerely objected to that term. But, judging not by conscious intentions but by historical consequences, he would have been wrong.

© RICHARD LOWENTHAL 1960

WILLI MUENZENBERG

By R. N. Carew Hunt

FROM THE OUTSET of the First World War Lenin had decided that the Second International was done for, and that it should be replaced by another based upon Marxist revolutionary principles. Throughout the war he persistently advocated this, though even among the extremists who constituted the so-called "Zimmerwald Group" he had found few supporters. The seizure of power by the Bolsheviks gave him his opportunity. But for this it is improbable that a new International would have been set up, while if it had been it is certain that he would not have been chosen to direct the operation. The Comintern, however, became a rallying point for extremist left-wing elements, and thus in one country after another Communist Parties arose as splinter groups which had broken away from the parent Social Democratic body. Indeed affiliation to the Comintern was made conditional upon this. The famous "Twenty-one Conditions" split the European labour movement as Lenin intended they should do.

As might have been foreseen, the result was that the members of the new parties were animated by a spirit of fanaticism. This would have been well enough had there existed such a revolutionary situation as would have enabled them to take over the "commanding heights" of a sovietized Europe. But this was not the position, and the Third Comintern Congress of June–July 1921 found itself compelled to recognize that capitalism had achieved a temporary stabilization, and that this called for a change of line embodied in the slogan now adopted of "To the masses".

The new policy took the form of the so-called United Front tactics, and it was formally introduced by Zinoviev at a meeting of the ECCI on December 4th, 1921. The object of these tactics was to enable Communist Parties to penetrate other workers' organizations with a view to securing control over them. It is, however, symptomatic of the temper of the movement that this proposal met with a hostile reception in France, Italy and Spain, where it was interpreted as being alike a sign of weakness and an abandonment of principle, thus proving that Lenin's *Left-wing Communism*, written in April 1920 and published on the eve of the Second Congress, had not succeeded in exorcising that sectarianism which led Communists to regard as anathema any collaboration with non-Communist and particularly with Social Democratic elements. Indeed the French party virtually refused to do what it was told, and it was not until an enlarged Plenum of the ECCI was held under Trotsky's chairmanship on March 4th, 1922, that it came into line. The adoption of the United Front tactics amounted to the admission that Communism, so far from spreading like a prairie fire, was likely to encounter a long and stubborn resistance, and that new and more effective proselytizing methods would have therefore to be employed. But side by side with this was a dawning recognition of the fact that the movement would make no rapid progress if it was fostered only by such organizations as were avowedly Communist, or which the Communists sought to render so; and that these must be reinforced by others which would appeal to sections of the community which were not at all prepared to accept Communism, but which regarded with sympathy one or other particular objective which the movement had an interest in promoting. It was to win over these peripheral elements that there were created the various Communist front organizations which aimed either at advancing some particular cause such as anti-imperialism, or at uniting a professional group such as lawyers and scientists, or at mobilizing some section of the community such as students. The emergence of these "fronts" cannot indeed be traced to any single positive decision, for their origin was in a sense undesigned. But their development and the increasingly important role they came to exert was primarily due to the genius of Willi Muenzenberg, the subject of this paper, who has been described as the patron saint of the "fellow-traveller".

But first a word as to sources. Muenzenberg's activities were so widespread and he had such a range of contacts that it is surprising that there are not more references to him in books written by Communists and ex-Communists. The fullest account of him in English is in Arthur Koestler's *The Invisible Writing*. Ruth Fischer, who knew him well, gives a brief sketch of him in her *Stalin and German Communism*, and I had quite recently an opportunity of discussing him with her. Then I have the notes of a long conversation I had some years ago with Muenzenberg's widow Babette Gross; and of another with her sister Margareta who married the German activist Heinz Neumann (organizer of the Canton commune and liquidated in the Great Purge). Ruth Fischer maintains that Babette did not play the important role in her husband's work that is sometimes ascribed to her, and also that her memory has been overlaid by the events of the War and the post-war years. Both Babette and Margareta Buber-Neumann have long been vehemently anti-Stalinist; and although they do not deny, as they could scarcely do, that Muenzenberg was for many years one of the most prominent members of the Comintern, they do their best to exhibit him in the role of a patriotic German, mainly concerned at least after 1933 in combating Fascism. The man who could have told us much was Muenzenberg's secretary, and general factotum, Hans Schultz. But he died early in 1938, without apparently having published any memoir.

Muenzenberg was born at Erfurt in Thuringia on August 14th, 1887. According to Buber-Neumann, his father ill-treated him as a child, and his attendance at school was irregular though he read everything he could lay his hands on. The only incident related of his early life is that at the age of twelve he ran away in order to enlist as a volunteer with the Boers, but he was caught and brought home. On his father's death he obtained work in a shoe factory, but later drifted to Switzerland with a view to study and was employed by a chemist in Zurich. But he had early been associated with the Socialistische Jugendverland. When war broke out in August 1914 Switzerland became the head-quarters of that organization and Muenzenberg its secretary general.

During these years Muenzenberg made the acquaintance of Lenin, Krupskaya, Zinoviev, Radek and Manuilsky, all of whom were in exile, and Lenin, who quickly recognized his ability, channelled his vague radicalism into practical revolutionary activity. In April 1915 his youth organization convened a conference at Berne which adopted a pacifist and anti-war attitude, and he published a journal, of which between September 1915 and May 1918 eleven numbers appeared, con-taining contributions by Lenin and other members of the Zimmerwald Group. In 1918 he was deported from Switzerland for subversive activities, and transferred his organization to Stuttgart. In November 1919, at a congress in Berlin, it reconstituted itself under his presidency as the Communist Youth International, in accordance with an appeal for such an organization which Zinoviev had launched in the name of the ECCI in the previous May. According to its programme, it was to be, however, an independent organization, though one which would conform to the political line of the Comintern. Muenzenberg attended the Second Comintern Congress, but was apparently unable to get it to discuss the new movement. None the less it prospered, and claimed on its first birthday a membership of 800,000 coming from 45 national youth organizations. When therefore it held its second congress at Jena in April 1921, the Comintern had become alive to its importance. At the same time the ECCI issued peremptory instructions that the Jena discussions were to be regarded as "not binding", and the congress be transferred to Moscow, where the Third Comintern Congress was scheduled to take place in June. This congress Muenzenberg attended and was rewarded with a seat on the ECCI. Zinoviev's report devoted considerable attention to the Youth International, which held its own congress immediately after that of the Comintern. At this there seem to have been some differences of opinion as to the status of the new International, but they were overcome. Its headquarters were transferred to Moscow where all its congresses were in future to be convened. Muenzenberg himself was not re-elected secretary, but was moved on to other work.

Buber-Neumann says that Zinoviev dropped Muenzenberg because he wanted someone more subservient, and that although the latter remained faithful to the Comintern for many years, it was this that sowed the first seeds of his ultimate disillusionment with Comintern methods. However, Ruth Fischer maintains that Muenzenberg, already a Reichstag deputy and a coming man, was naturally wanted for more important work. At the same time the new International had been his child, and it is thus unreasonable to suppose that the decision to relieve him of its custody cannot have been altogether welcome. But his new task provided even wider scope for his abilities.

The drought of the spring and summer of 1921 had led to a severe famine in Russia, and on June 26th *Pravda* admitted that twenty-five million people were starving. On July 13th Maxim Gorky launched a world-wide appeal for help, and on August 2nd Chicherin sent a circular note to the governments of Europe and the United States informing them of the extent of the disaster, and urging them not to interfere with any attempts made to mitigate it. Assistance was promptly forthcoming. Vast quantities of food and clothing were poured into Russia partly by the American Relief Association under Hoover's chairmanship, and partly by the Council for Russian Relief under Nansen, which had been set up in Geneva on August 15th by a committee sponsored by the Red Cross. To the value of their work the Commissar for Foreign Affairs paid tribute. None the less, it was felt desirable to reinforce these activities by others of a more specifically proletarian nature, and thus in September there was set up in Berlin, under Muenzenberg's chairmanship, the *International Workers' Aid*, generally referred to as the MRP, the initials of its Russian designation.

The importance of the MRP did not lie, however, in the tangible contribution it made to the relief of the famine, impressive as this undoubtedly was, but in the methods adopted. Muenzenberg had hit upon a new technique based on the simple observation that it is possible to persuade people to assist a cause in such a way that they become emotionally involved in it. Thus workers were asked to donate a day's wages, or alternatively to give whatever their factory produced —in one case knitting machines and in another milk separators, and to do so not as an act of charity towards the Russian people but rather as a gesture of solidarity with them. The propaganda value of this was out of all proportion to that of money collected or the goods supplied. The Comintern was quick to recognize the role that such organizations as the MRP could play, and it was to be the prototype of many others.

The famine ceased, but the MRP continued, and its paraphernalia of mobile canteens and soup kitchens made its appearance in other countries whenever this was held desirable in the interests of Communist propaganda—in Germany during the inflation, in Japan during the strikes of 1925, in England during the General Strike. At the same time, it ramified in innumerable directions, and became known as the "Muenzenberg Trust". By 1926 Muenzenberg owned two daily papers, *Berlin am Morgen* and *Welt am Abend*, the latter being the evening edition of the official party organ, *Rote Fahne*, and a weekly, the *Berliner Illustrierte Zeitung*, the Communist counterpart of the *Berliner Illustrierte* (an imitation of the American *Life*). How far these journalistic activities extended it is impossible to say, but according to Koestler, Muenzenberg owned or controlled nineteen magazines or newspapers in Japan alone, and what is more had made them pay. A further venture was a company with exclusive rights to distribute Soviet films, which had agents in London, Paris, Rome, Amsterdam and New York. But these were but parts of an elaborate apparatus linked up with banks, commercial and other institutions which not only propagated the Party line but also earned large sums for the movement.

Nor were Muenzenberg's activities confined to the MRP. He was also Secretary-General of the *League against Imperialism* founded in Brussels in February 1927, and denounced by the Socialist international in the following October as "nothing but a Communist manœuvre". Its statutes defined its objectives as "the union of all persons and organizations which, disregarding their own particular aims, are prepared to lend support in the struggle against imperialism and for the political and social liberation of all peoples"; and thus it secured the adhesion of many well-intentioned persons who were unaware that it was being used as cover for all sorts of Comintern activities. In December 1931 its headquarters in Berlin were raided by the police, who issued a report which established that it had throughout received its directives from the Comintern, that proposals made by non-Communist members of its governing body had invariably been side-tracked, that a number of members of its staff had forged passports or no passports at all, and that it possessed an intelligence apparatus with agents in various countries which reported in code to cover addresses. Its most active period was from 1927 to 1933 when the spotlight of Communist propaganda was directed to imperialist aggression as the inevitable prelude to a world war. When the Nazis came into power its headquarters were moved to Paris, as were those of most of Muenzenberg's "shows". After the Seventh Comintern Congress it was thought prudent to suspend it, but similar organizations with other names were set up in most countries, such as the *Colonial Information Bureau* which replaced it in Great Britain from 1937.

Also under Muenzenberg's direction was the *"Anti-Fascist Bureau"* which developed out of a congress held in Berlin in March 1929. When in the early thirties the political horizon began to darken as a result of the growing strength of the Nazis, it was decided that an anti-war campaign was desirable, and on August 27th, 1932, a congress met in Amsterdam of which Muenzenberg again was the controlling genius, though for the sake of appearances its ostensible direction was entrusted to the well-known French pacifist intellectuals, Henri Barbusse and Romain Rolland. It was attended by thousands of delegates, and was hailed as a "giant step" in the formation of organizations for the support of Russia. At a meeting in the Salle Pleyel in June 1933 the Committee of Action set up in Amsterdam were converted into the *"World Committee against War and Fascism"*—the most powerful of all the anti-fascist movements.

In the case of all these organizations care was naturally taken to represent them as spontaneous and independent of Moscow, and it was therefore regarded as undesirable that they should contain more than a leavening of Communists. The most effective arrangement was found to be to appoint as president a politically colourless but otherwise very prominent non-Communist, assisted by a committee of persons similarly qualified, and with a Communist or crypto-Communist in the background who exercised the required control. Apart from their primary function of manipulating public opinion along lines which suited Communist or Russian interests, these organizations provided promising recruiting grounds, and could also be used as cover for illegal activities, or even for the party itself were it to be declared illegal.

While therefore the official Communist Parties sought to capture the masses by frontal assault, the Communist "fronts" aimed at acting by indirect means that section of society which Soviet propaganda describes as the "progressive bourgeoisie". There were, in the thirties, many whose violent antipathy to Fascism made them increasingly sympathetic towards Communism. As Muenzenberg put it, "We must organize the intellectuals." He was himself peculiarly qualified to direct this operation. For apart from organizational ability of the highest order, and a mind which was forever thinking up new projects, he was a born leader who knew how to pick able subordinates and get the best out of them. Buber-Neumann says that his enemies accused him of choosing men who were out of favour with their parties as suspected deviationists, and in this there may be an element of truth, since those who did not share the rigid dogmatism of the ordinary Party *apparatchik* were likely to be of more use to him.

Buber-Neumann goes on to say, however, that Muenzenberg was unpopular with his party, and I have come across similar reports elsewhere. Ruth Fischer declared this to be nonsense. The importance of his work, she said, was fully recognized by the leaders and they were prepared to leave him to get on with it. This may have been true of the early years, but later, when the party had become Bolshevized, it certainly was not. Muenzenberg himself had always been careful not to take sides in party disputes, supporting those who were in power while maintaining friendly relations with those who were not. But this did not affect the fact that he worked outside the party framework as the nature of his operations obliged him to do. He had excellent connections in Moscow, particularly with Zinoviev and Kamenev, and enjoyed over many years a greater degree of freedom than any other Comintern agent. Thus he did not belong to any of the central organs of his party until the so-called Brussels Congress of 1935, which in fact was held in Moscow, when he was elected to the Central Committee of the KPD, apparently on the initiative of Pieck. The Popular Front policy had just been officially proclaimed at the Seventh Comintern Congress and the KPD had been hauled over the coals in Moscow for not having applied it earlier, though to have done so would have been contrary to the party line. In view of Muenzenberg's multifarious contacts with anti-fascist circles, the decision to bring him on to the Central Committee appears therefore natural enough. Yet this may not have been the only motive for so doing. Here was a man who was running, very much as a free-lance, what almost amounted to a private Comintern of his own, and one which was mushrooming in every direction. It is unlikely that the new type of Stalinist leader such as Ulbricht would have regarded this with favour, and it may well have been felt that as a member of what was at the time the highest executive party organ he would be more amenable to control.

It was clear that there would be no room for Muenzenberg in Hitler's Germany. In late February 1933, just about the time of the Reichstag Fire, he disappeared. In April he was reported to have been seen in Paris, where Barbusse was said to be looking after him; and in the same month he obtained a *permis de séjour* from the French Ministry of the Interior. Thereafter he became the leader of the Communist anti-fascist campaign, and Goebbels' principal antagonist, for which he was condemned to death *in absentia* in 1935, his wife receiving the same sentence three years later. The story of his activities is told in some detail by Koestler, who joined his staff when the Leipzig Fire trial started in September 1933, and was associated for a time with what was the latest of Muenzenberg's shows, *The Committee for the Relief of the Victims of German Fascism*. This had branches all over Europe and in America, and was supported, as Koestler points out, by innumerable respectable persons who had never heard of Muenzenberg, and believed the Comintern to be a bogey invented by Goebbels. To assist its operation Muenzenberg founded a new publishing firm—*Editions du Carrefour*—which put out a spate of propaganda literature, one of the most sensational items of which was *The First Brown Book of the Hitler Terror and the Burning of the Reichstag*, actually written by Otto Katz, a talented journalist who was Muenzenberg's principal executive. It was translated into many languages, and large numbers of copies found their way into Germany under innocent sounding titles. Its thesis was that the Reichstag Fire, so far from being the signal for a Communist uprising, as Goebbels maintained, was an act of provocation planned by Roehm and his SA group with a view to discrediting the KPD.

This may indeed have been true, though the evidence for it was scarcely conclusive enough to warrant the categorical statements made. The book however was aimed at that large class of reader which is not very interested in the distinction between assertion and proof, especially if its sympathies are already engaged. Further, it was through Muenzenberg and Katz that the question of the responsibility for the fire was investigated in London at a "shadow trial" in which a number of lawyers of international reputation took part and at which the Communists were duly acquitted. Thus by the time of the Leipzig Trial, the issue had already been adjudged in the court of world public opinion.

Buber-Neumann, who professes to be reprinting private conversations, declares that after the severance of his connection with the Youth International, Muenzenberg's interests became centred on Western Europe, and that he early realized the dangers inherent in Russian control of the Comintern. At first he had shared the general belief that the revolution would speedily engulf all Europe, and it had been Paul Levi who had first administered a douche of cold water by pointing out that the capitalist system was much stronger than Moscow chose to admit, and that no crisis was likely to occur for at least ten years—a view to which the failure of all revolutions attempted in Europe lent support. Buber-Neumann admits, however, that at least up to 1933, whatever doubts he may have entertained did not affect his loyalty to the Comintern; though he was to become thereafter increasingly assailed by them. It was indeed some years before they created such a tension as to lead him to break with the Communist movement. Yet this is no unusual phenomenon seeing that with convinced party members the decision to renounce Communism is commonly the result of a long period of incubation. Certainly the policy of the Comintern in the period, which led up to the victory of the Nazis, and the complete collapse of the KPD, and incidentally the dislocation of his own organization which had been based on Berlin, was not calculated to strengthen his faith in Moscow's infallibility. Moreover in Paris he found himself in an atmosphere more critical than that to which he had been hitherto accustomed, and Buber-Neumann may be correct in saying that he began for the first time to be aware of the existence of a body of anti-Marxist-Leninist literature and to study it.

Yet whether he was much influenced may be doubted. His position in the years that followed is clear enough. He had a thorough knowledge of Germany and of the danger of German militarism, and was determined to oppose Nazism by every means in his power. The question was how far the Comintern, or Stalin, who directed its policies, was prepared to do the same. The language of vituperation with which Moscow and Berlin were attacking one another reflected a genuine ideological divergence. But when two great powers are neighbours ideology does not always have the last word. The Soviet Union was bound to Germany by more links than one, and Stalin was not strong enough to risk a rupture. The policy that was now adopted was that of the Popular Front, officially proclaimed at the Seventh Comintern Congress of the summer of 1935, though it had in fact already been adopted by the French CP. This was all very well as far as it went. The view has been expressed that the Popular Front could only have been made really effective if the Comintern were dissolved; and Stalin was not yet prepared for this.

After the Seventh Congress came the purges. First, the trial of Zinoviev, Kamenev and the so-called "Leningrad Centre" in August 1936; secondly, that of Radek, Piatakov, Muralov and fourteen others in January 1937; thirdly, that of Tukachevsky and six Red Army generals in June 1937; and finally that of Bukharin, Rykov, Yagoda and others in March, 1938. Shortly after the Zinoviev trial Muenzenberg attended a peace conference in Amsterdam, and in the street ran into a former friend, Sneevliet, by this time a Trotskyist, who under the alias of Maring had founded the Indonesian Communist Party in 1920 and had negotiated the famous alliance between the Chinese Communist Party and the Kuomintang of 1922. Sneevliet shouted at him, "You traitor Cain, where is Zinoviev, your brother Abel?" It is true that by no justifiable stretch of imagination could Muenzenberg be held responsible for Zinoviev's fate. None the less Buber-Neumann declares that he was deeply affected by this incident. Yet he and Babette left in September for Moscow, the ostensible reason for the visit being that Manuilsky wanted him to report personally on his work, and to discuss a proposal, which had apparently been revived, that he should give up his work in Paris and become Agitpropleiter of the YCI. Babette told me that this suggestion had come from the Comintern Secretary-General Dimitrov, made by either or by both. That it may have been meant seriously is suggested by the fact that in the summer the Czech Communist Smeral had been sent to Paris to make himself thoroughly acquainted with Muenzenberg's affairs.

At the time of Muenzenberg's visit Heinz Neumann and his wife were in Moscow. The latter was in trouble with the KPD for having led an opposition movement against the party leader Thälmann, and was destined to disappear in the purges, while she was to be sent to a concentration camp until she was handed over to the Gestapo after the Stalin–Hitler Pact. She is therefore a good witness for this particular episode in her brother-in-law's life. She declares that he knew that he was regarded with suspicion in Moscow, and that his motive for going there at so critical a time was his desire to obtain Russian support for the Spanish Loyalists. The Civil War had started on July 16th, and del Vayo, later to become Foreign Minister in the Negrin Government, and the Spanish Ambassador in Paris, Araquistain, had both appealed to him for help in what seemed to all to be a clear issue with fascism. Muenzenberg who, to quote Koestler, produced committees as a conjuror produces rabbits out of a hat, had therefore set up the *Committee for War Relief for Republican Spain*, thus using, as in the case of Germany, philanthropic cover for political operations; and this body was soon supplemented by the *Committee of Inquiry into Foreign Intervention in the Spanish Civil War* which performed a service somewhat similar to that of the Reichstag counter-trial. Having thus deeply involved himself in pro-Loyalist activities, he could not refuse the Comintern's invitation.

Shortly after his arrival in Moscow, Muenzenberg was summoned before the International Control Commission, the organ of the Comintern responsible under Art. 28 of the Constitution of 1928 for "matters connected with the Communist conduct of individual members of the various Sections", or in other words for taking disciplinary action when necessary. He was questioned about certain persons employed in his Paris office, and in particular about a shorthand typist called Liane who was now alleged to be a spy of Franco's. At first Muenzenberg refused to take this seriously, but when the matter was raised a second and then a third time, he began to be uneasy, and to suspect that he was in the hands of the NKVD. Then he became aware that a rumour was going around that he had offended against "revolutionary vigilance" and that he was being avoided by his friends. A request that he should remain in Moscow now became an order to do so. But Muenzenberg was not going to stand this, and insisted that before there could be any question of his settling in Moscow he must first be allowed to return to Paris and clear up his various commitments. Manuilsky appeared to concur, and a date was actually fixed for the journey. For this he required an exit permit and a visa, and the practice at that time was not to hand these to the departing visitor until he arrived at the station.

But when on the appointed day the Muenzenbergs were waiting for their train, a messenger arrived who told them that the permit was not available as the visa had been refused. Thus they returned to their hotel in despair. On the next day, however, Muenzenberg tackled Togliatti, who was temporarily deputizing for Dimitrov, and Buber-Neumann declares that he succeeded in winning him over. What is possible is that Togliatti or someone else pointed out that as Stalin had now decided to support the Spanish Loyalists, Muenzenberg's organization could render valuable services. However this may be, he secured his visa and left Moscow twenty-four hours later.

The story now becomes somewhat difficult to unravel as the evidence is conflicting. We do not know the exact date of Muenzenberg's departure from Moscow. But Buber-Neumann says that as soon as he got back to France he had a nervous breakdown, and that he went into a clinic run by a certain Professor Chateaubriand. She adds that Bukharin had been there a year or two earlier, and that Chateaubriand, who had a Russian wife, had warned him against returning to Russia —advice which had been disregarded. She says, however, that even before he went into the clinic Muenzenberg handed everything over to Smeral, and Babette told me that he did this before the end of the year. According to her sister, he was careful to obtain receipts which could be produced if the Comintern later brought any charge against him. These highly compromising documents Babette deposited in the safe of a Catholic press agency which prudently burnt them when the Germans entered Paris; so that when the Gestapo searched the premises they found nothing. If the above is correct it would suggest that Muenzenberg's unfortunate experience in Moscow led him to sever his connection with the Comintern as soon as he returned to Paris. It may be, however, that he did not immediately do so, and that in handing over to Smeral he was simply acting in pursuance of a decision taken earlier in the year that he should be transferred to other duties. The first clear statement that he had finished with the Comintern that I have come across is in an article published in the newspaper Paul Miliukov was then editing in Paris—*Poslyedniya Novosti*—of July 26th, 1937. According to this, Muenzenberg had been in Moscow in the previous September, but although he had returned to Paris much depressed by the Zinoviev affair, there had been no disagreement between him and Dimitrov in regard to Comintern policy. A friend of his, a certain Sauerfeld, had remained in Moscow to act as his link with the Comintern. After the Radek trial of January 1937 he had been summoned back to refute charges of Trotskyism. He did not refuse to go, but kept putting his journey off, and in April entered a clinic. Meanwhile Sauerfeld, whose role seems in fact to have been that of a hostage for Muenzenberg's good behaviour, had been arrested as a Trotskyist and collaborator with the Gestapo. In June Muenzenberg was again summoned to Moscow, but this time refused. He wanted to go to the United States, but was unable to obtain a visa. As there were large sums of Comintern money standing in his name in banks in Amsterdam, Strassburg and Basle, Pieck had been to Paris to negotiate their transfer, but Muenzenberg refused to hand them over unless he was first given an assurance that Sauerfeld would be released. What was the outcome was not stated, but the article declared that Muenzenberg had not broken with the Comintern.

A second report, also from Paris and dated a few days later stated that Muenzenberg had been in difficulties with the Comintern, and had refused to go to Moscow. He had been told that if he did not do so, he would be dismissed not only from the Central Committee of the KPD but also from the party, and he had retaliated by threatening to publish his extensive knowledge of the Comintern's secret activities. It had therefore been decided that he should retain his party status, but his work had been taken over partly by the Hungarian Communist Bruno Freistadt and partly by Walter Ulbricht. Smeral is not mentioned. A third report, dated a few days earlier, declared that he had made a person appeal to Stalin, who was said to view the Comintern with disfavour (as indeed was true at the time), in which he had attacked Dimitrov.

Professor Kantorowicz, who served with the International Brigade, told me that he was surprised to learn that Muenzenberg had abandoned his Comintern operations as early as the end of 1936, as he believed him to be still actively concerned in pro-Loyalist activities during 1937. It may be that Buber-Neumann and Babette are somewhat unduly anxious to get him out of the Comintern at the earliest possible moment. But as to precisely when he severed his connection with that organization neither is wholly explicit; and all that Buber-Neumann has to say is that up to Christmas 1937 he kept on receiving summonses to Moscow, that he ignored them, and that, as she puts it, "with this his breach with the Comintern became finally complete". We are therefore left to assume that it took place at some time during that year. As for the transfer to Smeral, Ruth Fischer told me that it was little more than a formality. The success of Muenzenberg's organization she maintained was due to his personality, and when he was no longer there to direct it, it crumbled to pieces. Apart from this judgement, Smeral was in no state to preside over such an empire as he was in an advanced stage of diabetes.

What, however, appears strange at first sight is why the Moscow leaders should have wished to get rid of a man who was by far the most successful exponent of the "united front" policy of appealing to all-anti-fascist elements which they had themselves so recently proclaimed. But quite apart from Muenzenberg's contacts with Old Bolsheviks involved in the purges, it must be remembered that in proportion as Stalinist totalitarianism developed in the Soviet Union and was reflected in the leadership of the Comintern Sections, men of his type could no longer be tolerated. Babette told me that from about the time when he returned from Russia he began to be attacked by the KPD, as a "right deviationist", and that this in conjunction with the continuance of the purge trials made him unwilling to visit Moscow in January 1937 when summoned there by Dimitrov, to whom he had written setting out his objections. Dimitrov had replied that the trouble with the party could be cleared up, but Muenzenberg was not to be persuaded, doubtless realizing that in attacking a man in his position, the KPD was taking its cue from Moscow. Kantorowicz declared that when he was working with Muenzenberg, that is, before leaving for Spain, the latter had openly complained that he could do far more were he not continually hampered by interference from the party, and that this was his opinion would assuredly have been known in Moscow. Koestler says that Katz had been put in by the NKVD to spy on him and that he was perfectly aware of this. I asked Ruth Fischer whether she believed that Katz had been an agent, and she said that while he might have been she could not be sure. However, when I consulted her book on German Communism, I found that she had there committed herself to a definite statement that he was. In this particular section of the book she is, however, clearly drawing upon Koestler. Kantorowicz could throw no light on the matter, but agreed with Koestler's low estimate of Katz. If the latter was an agent, fate eventually caught up with him as he was among those executed in 1952 in connection with the Slansky case, the charge brought against him being that he was a British spy, a saboteur and a Zionist agent.

On May 23rd, 1938, the *Deutsche Volkszeitung* published a resolution of the Central Committee of the KPD excluding Muenzenberg from the party for action contrary to party principles and for breaches of discipline. More specifically, he was charged with intriguing against the Popular Front policy and with refusing to carry out the party's directives. The above duly appeared in the Russian press. In the following November it was stated however that Moscow, concerned at the fate of the Franco-Soviet Pact, was now trying to rehabilitate him and had offered him a post in the Ministry of Propaganda which he had refused; but of this there is no confirmation.

After his breach with the Comintern Muenzenberg started a weekly paper, *Die Zukunft*, of which in the autumn of 1938 Koestler became for a time the editor. Apart from conducting anti-fascist propaganda it sought to unite the various groups which were now in exile, and to develop a programme against the day when the Hitlerist régime would disappear. How long Koestler was associated with it he does not say, but the paper continued to appear under the editorship of Thorman, a member of the Catholic Centre party, until the end of 1939 or early in 1940, by which time most of its staff had been interned.

When the war broke out Muenzenberg was protected by prominent French politicians, and was therefore not immediately interned. According to Buber-Neumann, who I suspect is simply following Koestler's account of the matter, he was sent a few days before the capitulation of France to a concentration camp at Chambarran, to the East of Lyons; whereas, according to what Babette told me, he went at the beginning of 1940 to what she described as a "depot" near Lyons —presumably in the same place—which must have been some military or quasi-military installation, as she said that he worked there as a civilian employee. On the approach of the German forces he was allowed to leave, and made off in the direction of Valence with the evident intention of getting to Marseilles. He was last seen alive in the village of St Antoine with three companions who had been at Chambarran with him. It is significant that the district was a stronghold of Communist militants. In this village Muenzenberg was told that in the hamlet a kilometre or so distant there was a car which he could use, and the party therefore set off thither along a path through the woods. Some weeks later Muenzenberg's body was found under a tree. Round his neck was a strand of steel cord, the rest of which was dangling from a branch. The position of the branch is stated to have ruled out suicide. Buber-Neumann says that it is unthinkable that a man of Muenzenberg's temperament should have taken his life; nor had he any reason to do so, as he only had to get to Marseilles where a rich Roumanian friend of his would have provided the money and documents required to enable him to leave the country.

When the news of Muenzenberg's death became known, the Russians with somewhat suspicious alacrity hastened to throw the blame upon the Gestapo. But the Gestapo would not have killed him out of hand; they would assuredly have first wished to interrogate him. Both Babette and Buber-Neumann, and indeed everyone whom I have had an opportunity to consult, are convinced that Moscow was responsible. Though whether the three companions (whose identity was never discovered) were NKVD agents, or local Party thugs, or merely decoys, remains an open question.

But while this was the end of Muenzenberg, it has been by no means the end of the front organizations—the "Innocents' Clubs" as he used to call them—which he had done so much to bring into existence. Most of those with which he was concerned have long since disappeared, but only to be replaced by others which perform more or less similar functions. So often has their true nature been exposed that people must indeed be simple to go on being taken in by them. But then the world is largely made up of simple people.

© R. N. CAREW HUNT 1960

SOCIALISM IN AMERICA

By Earl Browder

I

THE MOST authoritative study of socialism in America is, perhaps, the monumental two-volume symposium entitled *Socialism in American Life*. Produced by fourteen major contributors under the editorship of Donald Drew Egbert and Stow Persons for the Program in American Civilization at Princeton University, it has a greater unity than might be expected, and is a veritable treasure-house of systematic information as to what happened to the ideas of socialism when they were imported from Europe to America. The dominant assumption of the study is expressed in the first chapter, by E. H. Harbison, when he writes: "The study of American socialism begins in Europe." America made small contribution to the ideas of socialism, and this little of limited consequence. Socialism is dealt with as an ideology, or varieties of related ideologies, with roots primarily in Europe.

America makes no reciprocal impact upon socialism except, in the main, a negative one in refuting the ideology, first of the utopian and religious socialisms, and, later, of Marxism as it became dominant in the field of socialist thought. The picture is drawn of Marxism, while becoming over the last century a great and growing power in the rest of the world, in America suffering continuous decline and eventual dispersal. In America socialist ideology has become a negligible influence. From this viewpoint America has defeated socialism.

This is much too narrow a framework, however, to contain a broad historical view of socialism in relation to America. There is, among those features excluded, the fact that socialism radically challenges America for world leadership, thus transforming her environment; if socialism is no longer even a remote inner challenge, in its world role it has become the first effectual challenger with profound internal results upon America. The primitive level on which America responds, primarily by taking up an uncongenial and increasingly ineffectual military role, brings in its train a whole complex of new and unfamiliar problems. America is not equipped to understand these problems, and the rise of the socialist challenge in its Russian form is regarded consequently as something in the nature of an emanation of diabolical powers or witchcraft. This is the origin of McCarthyism, so puzzling to Europeans who face the problem on a more rational plane and cannot understand why the country to which socialism is the smallest practical inner challenge should be the most hysterical in facing it in the world. But indeed it is precisely the absence of an inner challenge that makes America somewhat irrational in facing it on the world stage. She feels as though she is fighting disembodied spirits as well as more earthly powers. Witch-hunting is a logical consequence.

There is another reason, probably more important in the long run, why the purely ideological framework is inadequate to deal with socialism in America. This is the fact that America defeated Marxism not by ideological struggle, but by pragmatically refuting its dogma of pauperization, through an unparalleled rate of accumulation of capital while advancing general living standards, and thus gave the most emphatic confirmation of the less-known Marxist laws of concentration and centralization of capital. The Marxist dogma that was refuted (pauperization) furnished merely the *subjective* base for positing a historical movement towards socialism; the laws that were confirmed provided the *objective* base, the "self movement of material reality", independently of men's ideas and, according to Marx's larger concept, in the long run destined to shape men's ideas. American reality thus, while knocking out one side of the Marxist dogma, was confirming the other side as something more than dogma. Since almost all attention was concentrated on the pauperization issue, what America was conscious of was primarily her victory over Marxism; while only a few scholars took note that simultaneously America was confirming the *objective* laws underlying the historical trend to socialism.

In America, under the form of privately-owned capital, concentration and centralization brought into being the most socially-organized productive process itself. The corporate form united private ownership of *share capital* with a wide social organization of production; the private owner no longer owned any unit of the means of production, but merely a paper claim to a *pro rata* share in the final accumulation of profits. Management itself was more and more divorced from ownership. The rise of trusts, ever-growing groupings of corporations, carried the process to a higher stage. Public control and regulation created a certain, if limited, transfer of the original exclusive proprietary rights of capital to the public, and opened up *unlimited potentialities* in this direction. Graduated income and inheritance taxes (first demanded in a political platform in the *Communist Manifesto*), established a growing public claim upon profit and accumulation superior to the private claim. Distribution as well as production was drawn into the socializing process, so that vast corporations dominate it. Today the overwhelming mass of American economic activity of all sorts is centralized in trusts or groups of corporations, uniting the largest mass of productive and distributive workers under unified direction, with the highest technique and rate of productivity, in the most integrated economy in the world. With one-eighth of the world's population, this economy's total yearly production still approximates that of the rest of the world, despite the startling advances of the USSR. So obviously superior is America's economic technique that Russia, despite its claims to *ultimate* superiority, readily admits America's immediate pre-eminence by adopting as its own goal the aim to *catch up with and surpass America.*

America, seen from this viewpoint, is therefore a living paradox, with the lowest degree of socialist ideology combined with the highest degree of socialization of the technique of the economy, especially production, and a rapidly expanding social appropriation of the national surplus. The sharp contrast between the capitalist and socialist systems becomes increasingly blurred when one passes from ideology to material reality, where the two giants of world power tend to resemble each other more and more with every passing year.

II

American economy brilliantly confirmed Marx's discovery of the laws of concentration and centralization of capital. But it was quite the opposite with Marx's doctrine of impoverishment or pauperization as the "absolute general law" of capital accumulation. America stood before the world as a refutation of the doctrine of impoverishment throughout her national history. The dogma is, indeed, the chief reason Marx failed to gain recognition in America as he did in Europe, and why American labour consciously struggled against Marxism before capitalists and intellectuals even realized that Marxism was a challenge.

The doctrine of impoverishment is the oldest component element of socialist ideology, with its roots in pre-capitalist society. Probably its most ancient expression is to be found in the Gospel according to St Matthew, chapter 25, the parable of the talents, culminating in the much-quoted verse 29: "For unto everyone that hath shall be given, and he shall have abundance; but from him that hath not shall be taken away even that which he hath." This ancient folk-wisdom foreshadowed the widely accepted doctrine of political economy, and also was a key thought in all schools of socialist ideology. For political economy it served to justify the economic *status quo* with the thought that poverty was the unavoidable product of natural (or divine) law, while for all schools of socialism it was the central motive for demanding a radical change in the economic system.

Marx gave the ancient doctrine, which he inherited in the political economy of his time, its more modern and scientific form and setting. Marx saw as the base or starting point for the capitalist mode of production, the fact of exclusion of the main population from the land, leaving a surplus or redundant population without means of livelihood except employment as wage labour. Here was the "industrial reserve army" upon which the nascent capitalist could draw for labourers at the cheapest possible price, namely, the subsistence of the labourer. With the development of more productive techniques that accompanies the accumulation of capital, antiquated modes of production, unable to compete, add to the surplus population those formerly employed in them, and the "industrial reserve army" increases at a greater rate than the increase of employment. The unemployed and partially employed fall into pauperism, which from being the starting point of capitalist accumulation has been transformed into its most characteristic product, so that pauperization is its "absolute general law". The same conclusion arises from an analysis of the "value" of labour or labour-power which, following Ricardo, is determined by the value of its cost of production, or subsistence. The ancient doctrine seems thus to be firmly anchored in the reality of capital-labour relation as well as in the theories of political economy.

So Marx thought for almost twenty years. But in 1865 he was shaken by doubts and second thoughts. Shortly before he finished and published *Capital* (the first volume), he found himself in a public controversy with a colleague named Weston, in the General Council of the International Workingmen's Association. Weston had raised and defended the idea that the working class could not improve its general position through increased wages, and had impressed the Council so much that Marx was uneasy lest Weston's position be approved. This, as he wrote Engels, would mean that "we should be turned into a joke" since the IWA was composed of trade unions fighting for better wages and shorter hours. After a month of preparations, Marx spoke for two nights to the General Council, to prove theoretically that trade unions could better the situation of the working class in more than a superficial and temporary sense.

In preparing for this task, however, Marx found it necessary to step outside the limits of the subsistence-wage theory and to break new ground. Besides the "physical limit" of subsistence he found it necessary to admit into the value of labour-power (not merely into the price, which might be a temporary deviation from value) also an additional increment of a historical, moral, or social origin. Here for the first time he went outside the limits of the theory he adopted from Ricardo in 1849, which hitherto he had refined and elaborated but had not broadened. In substance he demonstrated that trade unions could overcome the "absolute general law" of pauperization, and even that it could be overcome without large-scale trade union intervention.

But it was too late in Marx's life for him to revise his over-all theoretical system to conform to this new insight. Within two years he published *Capital* with the "absolute law" at the heart of its argument, and with only a fragment of his new look at wages of 1865 included. His report to the General Council gathered dust in his archives, and was not published until 1898, long after his more primitive theory of 1849 had been established as orthodox Marxist doctrine.

Marx had opened the door, but allowed it to be slammed shut again. He had missed his great opportunity to bring his general theory into harmony with the facts of American development. America refuted in living practice the doctrine of pauperization, as Marx well knew, and it continued to do so, which Marx did not expect. His basic mistake was that he took England as the "classic ground" whereon to discover the laws of capitalist development, when America had already displaced England in this role. In England he discovered, painfully and under extreme pressure, that subsistence need not be the controlling element in wages, that beside it there was another element (historical, moral, social) with enormous dynamic potentialities. But if he had recognized these elements in America, where they were so much more highly developed, he would have been forced to recast his entire theoretical system. Unfortunately for the realistic development of ideology, he thought of America as "still, economically speaking, only a colony of Europe", putting it aside as "exceptional", doomed to follow the laws he discovered in the older society. If he had taken America as the "norm" of capitalism, his main body of thought would have remained in all its grandeur, purged of those dogmas which have plagued socialist ideology from that day to the present. And America was obviously, a century ago, the "classic ground" of capitalism, its norm-creating centre.

III

It will be illuminating to take a closer, more detailed, look at Marx's report to the IWA in 1865. It contained all the key elements of a new wage theory which should immediately have subordinated the original dogma of subsistence as the ruling element in wages (or, more precisely, in the value of labour-power). The original dogma held with David Ricardo (along with the whole classical school of economists), that in the confrontation of capital with labour on the wages question, what one gains the other loses, what one loses the other gains. As most of them expressed it in almost identical words, "profits depend on high or low wages and on nothing else" (Ricardo), or "profits depend wholly on wages" (James Mill), or "profit rises to the extent that wages fall; it falls to the extent that wages rise" (Marx). But in his 1865 report Marx demonstrated an opposite principle. He showed that by means of a compulsory rise in the wage level, resulting from the Ten Hours Bill, not only had the conditions of English workers been tremendously bettered all around, with higher wages, shorter hours, more employment—but also that the employers had gained equally, with expanded productivity bringing lower costs and prices, wider markets, and expanded accumulation of capital. He had discovered in England, on a small scale, the same process that in America, on a large scale, was making her the strongest nation in the world economically. But in America Marx dismissed the higher wage level as an exceptional case, due to lack of capitalist development, and not a promise of higher development. In fact, in *Capital*, Marx specifically declared that America was, "speaking economically, still only a colony of Europe".

Marx never completed his 1865 excursion into new fields of wage theory. But he did discover all the essential elements of a new theory, which I have proposed to label "the social wage", which might have reconciled his larger theory of history with American experience. He revealed in the social increment in wages not only a measure of material civilization to which the given country had achieved, but also a new dynamic force that, far from hampering accumulation, stimulated technological advance and rising productivity, thus furnishing a base for expanded accumulation and still higher wages. He saw that "although we can fix the *minimum* of wages, we cannot fix their *maximum*". He departed, so far from the subsistence dogma as to say that in the struggle over wages "the question resolves itself into a question of the respective powers of the combatants". And if he continued to overestimate the power of the capitalist, as he clearly did at all times, that could have been corrected by further observation and analysis.

While Marx and Engels, during most of their adult lives, predicted eventual American supremacy in the capitalist world market, in which they proved quite correct, they expected this to occur through pauperization of the American workers, in which they were completely wrong. In the event it was high wages, rather than pauperization, that proved to be the "absolute general law" for America.

It seems especially strange that the two partners missed the larger significance of one phemonenon which they alone, among economists of their time, clearly noted and partially analysed. This is the fact that industrial inventions, whether of machinery or new applications of science in general, wherever they might originate, always tended to gravitate towards the country of highest wage levels for their practical application. Marx noted "the invention nowadays of machines in England that are used only in North America, just as in the sixteenth and seventeenth centuries machines were invented in Germany to be used only in Holland, and just as many a French invention of the eighteenth century was exploited in England alone". And Engels in similar vein wrote some years later that "the same implacable necessity that removed Flemish manufactures to Holland, Dutch ones to England, will ere long remove the centre of the world's industry from this country to the United States". In each case they were tracing a process of higher technology following the lead of higher wages, and thus shifting economic dominance from country to country.

From these and other considerations it should have been clear then, what has so well been proved in the result, that America had already replaced England as the "classic ground" from which to study the laws of capitalism. But Marx took England as that classic ground and, so far as the record shows, never doubted the soundness of that decision.

Just as he had discovered the elements of the social wage in England, but overlooked the fact that America raised these elements to a much higher stage, so also did he overlook the fact that America, by taking the lead in technology, was thereby setting the norm for world capitalism. What he labelled the "colony" was already becoming superior to the "metropolis", the tail was beginning to wag the dog. But Marx remained true to his original "model" and clung to the dogmas that were being proved unsound.

IV

In Marx's model or norm of capitalist society, the capitalists formed a "ruling class", relatively small and shrinking in ratio to total population, over the other classes and especially the working class, which was subjected, expanding in numbers but economically driven down to subsistence levels or below. The "ruling class" held state power, either directly or through servants, with the state as a sort of "executive committee" for the capitalists who were otherwise divided by ever-sharpening competition among themselves. Marx traced this "dictatorship" in society back to its foundation in the confrontation of capital versus labour, employer versus worker, in the struggle over division of the product in setting wage rates.

The employer controlling all means of production, as Marx saw it, held an overwhelmingly powerful position as against the worker, who had nothing but his labour-power to sell and a family that could eat only when he came to terms on wage-rates. Any little "freedom" the worker might have had in this bargaining was cancelled out by the industrial reserve army which, an automatic reservoir of "supply" for the capitalist's demand for labour-power, turned the law of supply and demand in favour of the capitalist. This, said Marx, "completes the despotism of capital", enables the employer to dictate the wage rate— a dictatorship which gradually engulfs society as a whole. The wage dictated by the capitalist will inevitably fluctuate around the norm of subsistence, or even below if the dictator does not fear a diminution of the labour force.

The development of machinery, with a consequent rise in the rate of productivity, turns the scale ever further in favour of the employer and against the worker. The power of the capitalist rises ever higher, that of the worker declines. The vicious circle is not capable of any gradual amelioration, it can only be broken by a single stroke when the working class, united and disciplined by the very production process, finally revolts, seizes the means of production and therewith the state power transforming it into a "dictatorship of the proletariat" until, some time in the undefined future, the state becomes unnecessary and "withers away". This is the model of class society as fixed by the Marxist dogmas, with the transition to socialism, long prepared and made inevitable by the inner laws of capitalism, coming as a cataclysmic "final conflict". The keystone of the whole structure is the original model of the confrontation of employer versus worker.

Whatever the defects of this model (and Marx himself revealed a few of them in his 1865 report), at least it makes a plausible and *prima facie* case with England as the classic ground. But it had little relation to the American example, and Marx could not possibly have constructed it on the basis of America. For it must be emphasized that Marx himself, from beginning to end of his economic studies, recognized that America stood outside this pattern. Marx only *predicted* that America would, sometime in the future, change to conform to the pattern. As early as 1846, for example, in a long letter to P. V. Annenkov concerning other matters, Marx remarked in passing that in America a primary motive for introducing machinery was "lack of hands", an implicit recognition of an inner dynamic quite different from that he traced in England from the base of a "stagnant surplus population". Furthermore, in 1865 in his debate with Weston, he wrote: "In colonial countries the law of supply and demand favours the working man. Hence the relatively high standard of wages in the United States. Capital may there try its utmost. It cannot prevent the labour market from being continuously emptied by the continuous conversion of wage labourers into independent, self-sustaining peasants." In America, thus, Marx himself found there was no "despotism" of capital over wages and, consequently, no "dictatorship" of the capitalists over society as a whole. The dogmatic Marxist model dissolves of itself, in the setting of America, and needs no refutation.

All of which, of course, in no way modifies the Marxist concept of the class struggle as a whole, but only its form and outcome. The elementary class struggle over wage rates was probably, over the past century, more turbulent in America than in England or Continental Europe. The big difference lies in the outcome of the struggle. In England Marx could comment, as a matter of course, that Adam Smith was correct when he said that in violent controversies over wages "the master is always master". But in America the opposite was obviously true, and the employer ("master") was never the master of wages. In America the workers won the primary dispute, and raised their wage level to about 2½ times that of England when Marx was writing. And whereas Marx expected this differential to swiftly disappear as capitalist industry rose to dominance and free land was exhausted, the opposite took place and, instead, it rose until it now stands at about 3½ to 1.

Marx considered that the capitalist system grew strong through victory of the capitalist over the worker on the wages question. America proved, to the contrary, that the realization of the full possibilities of capitalist production and accumulation required, as a precondition, that the capitalist should be defeated. American high wages led the way to technological superiority, which in turn gave America the dominant position over all rivals in the capitalist world market. In those lands where the capitalists were more able to have their way, the consequence was that the economy was stunted and dwarfed in comparison with America.

V

The concept of a capitalist ruling class derives from precapitalist society where political rights were the exclusive possession of certain limited "orders", the upper crust of society, clergy, landed gentry, the royal houses and their retainers skilled in the exercise of state power. With the rise of capitalism to dominance, Marx traced with great shrewdness and brilliance its influence in destroying the very fabric of the old order—but he assumed, for purposes of his theory, that the rising capitalist class would take over the state power and exercise it in an analogous manner.

In such a brief study as this one, it is impossible to examine in detail the degree of conflict and of correspondence between this Marxist concept and the complex reality of England and Europe. The main points must be made from American experience, where the concept of "ruling class" breaks down most completely and clearly. However, it is worth noting that Marx and Engels themselves, in dealing with current historical events in their own time, tended to ignore the dogma of a ruling class, and seized upon their materials in all their complexity without the aid of this simplifying formula. They even came forth with some broad general conclusions that flatly denied it.

For example, Engels in an introduction to the first English edition of *Socialism: Utopian and Scientific* (published as an article in the German *Neue Zeit*, 1892–3), said:

"It seems a law of historical development that the bourgeoisie can in no European country get hold of political power—at least for any length of time—in the same exclusive way in which the feudal aristocracy kept hold of it during the Middle Ages. Even in France, where feudalism was completely extinguished, the bourgeoisie, as a whole, has held full possession of the government for very short periods only. . . . In England the bourgeoisie never held undivided sway."

Neither Marx nor Engels fully understood democracy as it developed in England and, especially, in America. They scorned it as a fraud, as merely another if more complicated means of tricking the masses into serving the capitalists. But there were occasions when even these debunkers of democracy paid sincere tribute to its contributions to human progress. One recalls, for example, how Marx in a letter to Danielson (translator of *Capital* into Russian), in 1879, eulogizes American progress as contrasted with Russian degeneration; he balances this off a bit by saying that in America also there is a "gradual expropriation of the masses", but then notes that in America "the masses are quicker, and have greater political means in their hands, to resent the form of a progress accomplished at their expense". Thus, though he saw no economic counter-influence to expropriation, he did see a political one—which is exactly the reality of democracy.

Engels made an analogous tribute to English democracy, in the article last quoted. Here, after noting "that barbarous feudal language" in which it is preserved, he goes on to say:

"That same English law is the only one which preserved through the ages, and transmitted to America and the colonies, the best part of that old Germanic personal freedom, local self-government and independence from all interference but that of the law courts, which on the Continent has been lost during the period of absolute monarchy, and has nowhere been as yet fully recovered."

One might also note that almost naïve appeal Marx addressed to "the classes that are for the nonce the ruling ones" in Germany, in the preface to the first edition of *Capital*. He appeals to them to recognize that "their own most important interests dictate . . . the removal of all legally removable hindrances to the free development of the working class". He says that conditions in Germany are much worse than in England "because the counter-poise of the Factory Acts is wanting". Therefore Germany suffers from the incompleteness of capitalist development, "we suffer not only from the living but from the dead". There is no doubt that Marx gave good advice to those "ruling classes" in Germany, even if they did not see fit to follow it.

Even that most dogmatic of Marxists in evaluating the West, Vladimir Lenin, writing before the war around 1908, recognized the reality and positive qualities of American democracy in terms which cannot be squared with his *State and Revolution* or the later dogmas of the Communist International. One quotation, from among many, will serve. Lenin said:

"The foremost country of modern capitalism is particularly interesting for the study of the social-economic structure and evolution in modern agriculture. The United States is unequalled in rapidity of development of capitalism at the end of the nineteenth and beginning of the twentieth century, in the high level of development already attained, in the vastness of its territory—on which is employed the most up-to-date technical equipment suitable for the remarkable variety of natural and historical conditions—and in the degree of political freedom and the cultural level of the masses of the people. Indeed, this country is in many respects the model and ideal of our bourgeois civilization."

Thus the dogmas of the "ruling class" and of "dictatorship", dominating the Marxist theoretical system, do so only by flatly disregarding the contradictory facts recognized and described by the founders and most distinguished disciples of Marxism themselves. These observations testify to the reality of democracy, and the absence of class dictatorship; the dogma denies that reality and tags democracy as a fraud, a mask to hide the dictatorship of the bourgeoisie. America has never been able to see the valid and valuable aspects of the thought of Marx, because its view was obstructed by these obviously mistaken dogmas.

VI

There was a moment in history when it looked, for a while, as though Marx was about to gain recognition in America. This was the period of the Great Economic Crisis of 1930-4. That was the most shocking experience in American history, far deeper than any war. All the conventional index figures of economic life were at high point when the crisis broke over the nation. Few paid any attention at that time to certain divergent lines, with rate of productivity going up sharply, wage rates steady or even downward, and employment going down almost as productivity went up. Even fewer realized that the flood of speculative capital on the stock market had been diverted from investment in new means of production, because they were fascinated by the torrent of paper "profits" churned up by frenzied speculation. The crisis came like a bolt of lightning from a clear sky. It was a visitation by an angry God. In depth and duration the crisis went beyond anything in previous experience. It shook the dominant ideological structure even more than the economy. For the first time the leading strata of all classes were deprived over a period of years of the traditional American confidence that progress "onward and upward forever" was their destiny.

Intellectual America in this crisis period, under conditions of shock, discovered Marx the prophet of doom for capitalism. "Pauperization" of a sort struck overnight even in the families of Wall Street bankers, so no one laughed any more at Marx's "absolute general law" of pauperization, but looked upon it with almost superstitious awe. The ghost of Marx, not very clearly defined but nevertheless potent, assumed a sort of "hegemony" over the intellectual life of the 1930's, and even those who resisted it were shaped by it, and made concession after concession to it. If only because there was no rival coherent effort at an over-all explanation of the disaster, Marx, or at least his apocalyptic spirit, took over and set the norms of intellectual conformity.

Among men of practical affairs the search for a reform programme was fumbling, and much disturbed by the thought expressed by one bright young man who named his current book *Farewell to Reform!* And when F. D. Roosevelt won the election in 1932, it was not on a programme but on a slogan—"a new deal"—around which the new administration painfully gathered a programme through trial and error, over several years. Hitler took power in Germany almost simultaneously with Roosevelt in America. Until 1935 Roosevelt's administration had within it a powerful current of thought that accepted Hitler as the type representing the future; this was defeated not so much by counter-ideas as by the sudden emergence of a new mass force in the labour movement, the way for which had been opened

up by an obscure paragraph in the NRA (National Recovery Act),
Section 7a, legally recognizing collective bargaining as a *right* of labour.
The wave of unionization that swept the hitherto unorganized mass
production industries gave Roosevelt an independent mass base in
politics, and eliminated the pro-Hitler trend. By 1936 the New Deal
had definitely crystallized into a far-reaching movement of social
reform. The "left-of-centre" coalition around Roosevelt that thereafter dominated the 1930's, included as not-too-comfortable bed-
fellows both the revolutionarily-inspired intellectuals and the down-to-
earth reformers most strongly represented by the new mass labour
movement.

The American Communist party's role in the 1930's is perhaps the
most complex factor, most difficult to evaluate in retrospect, and therefore a very controversial subject. A few characteristic features, however, seem to be indisputable. Entering the 1930's as a small ultra-left
sect of some 7,000 members, remnant of the fratricidal factional struggle
of the 1920's that had wiped out the old "left wing" of American
socialism, the CP rose to become a national political influence far
beyond its numbers (at its height it never exceeded 100,000 members),
on a scale never before reached by a socialist movement claiming the
Marxist tradition. It became a practical power in organized labour, its
influence became strong in some state organizations of the Democratic
Party (even dominant in a few for some years), and even some Re-
publicans solicited its support. It guided the anti-Hitler movement
of the American League for Peace and Democracy that united a cross-
section of some five million organized Americans (a list of its sponsors
and speakers would include almost a majority of Roosevelt's Cabinet,
the most prominent intellectuals, judges of all grades up to State
Supreme Courts, church leaders, labour leaders, etc.). Right-wing
intellectuals complained that it exercised an effective veto in almost all
publishing houses against their books, and it is at least certain that
those right-wingers had extreme difficulty getting published. It displaced the old Socialist Party of Norman Thomas as the dominant
influence on the left, and that party split up during the 1930's. Beginning the period as an ultra-left sect, expressing the extremism of the
"third period" and "social-fascism" doctrines of the Communist International, it gradually merged with the organized labour movement
and the New Deal in all practical activities, while retaining the façade
of orthodox Marxism for ceremonial occasions. It became the most
successful reformist party in the Marxist tradition that America had

seen, while remaining unchallenged as the spokesman of revolutionary Marxism in its ideological aspects. While championing the Soviet Union in international affairs, it turned to the Jeffersonian American tradition as equally authoritative as that of Marx, in the same years when the bourgeois intellectuals were so preoccupied with Marx and Russia that the finest book they produced in the whole period was Edmund Wilson's brilliant if somewhat erratic *To the Finland Station*. The American CP was doubtless for years a severe headache to the ideologists of the Kremlin (although American intellectuals blindly insisted it was a puppet of Stalin), but the Russians silently tolerated it during the years of Hitler rule over Germany, because the results of its unorthodox work were so obviously favourable to Russian interests. But before the war was over, as soon as Hitler's defeat was assured, the Russians speedily brought this anomaly to an end; they denounced the CP's reformist course and called American Communists back to Leninist–Stalinist orthodoxy. The result was to shatter the American movement. Today nothing is left but a few fragments, museum pieces, and a collection of memories concerning which few persons find agreement. The "Indian summer" of Marxism in America could not outlive the World War.

VII

American capitalism emerged from its greatest crisis, shaken but unbroken. It accomplished this with the zealous assistance of the American Marxists, who fought passionately and with some degree of effectiveness, for the very measures which removed any reasons for a violent socialist revolution on the model of dogmatic Marxism.

A trickle of reforms became so popular, and so much stimulated the economy, that it turned into a steady stream. Indeed it may be said that the gamut of social legislation that took fifty years to mature in England and Scandinavia until it became possible to speak of "the welfare state", were adopted in America in the course of ten years and on a higher scale. Here the double question arises, why the delay in America which was so much more advanced economically, and why the speed once the process began?

The delay in American reforms was due to an ideological block, as well as the fact that expansion of the economy had relieved the most urgent necessities for reform until the crisis came. Past successes tended to confirm old ideologies, and a big majority of Americans looked with suspicion upon any enlargement or expansion of state functions (and still do so more than Europeans). Even the official leadership of the American Federation of Labor opposed the adoption of unemployment insurance and old-age retirement pensions until 1935, when it awoke to the fact that its membership was deserting it on this issue, at which time it promptly reversed its stand; social insurance became law before the year was over. This example of the A.F. of L. shows the cause of both the delay and the eventual speed. The reforms were overdue. Profits and accumulation after the first World War were outgrowing distribution so that reinvestment in new productive capital began to lag more and more, and idle capital turned to speculation. Capitalists had grown too strong for their own good, not to speak of the good of the nation. The depth of the 1929–34 crisis drove this lesson home. Once the ideological block against reforms was broken down or eroded by the crisis, reforms followed in a flood.

The reformers always insisted that their aims were conservative, to save the established system. The opponents of reform always insisted that it was step-by-step revolution, and one anonymous genius called the New Deal "creeping socialism"—which became a rallying battle-cry for the reactionary camp. This idea brought up to date is now being broadcast by an association of electric power corporations, fighting against expansion of government-owned hydro-electric facilities, in a series of advertisements to the public; under the headline "Is the U.S. Buying Socialism on the Installment Plan?", it gives the answer that "There's clear evidence that socialism is being sold to Americans on time."

Both sides are correct in this dispute. The *intention* behind reform is almost always conservative, but the *result* of reforms carried to a certain degree can amount in substance to a revolution. This becomes especially evident when reforms are scaled to the American economy. For example, unemployment insurance is woefully inadequate when measured against the American production potential; but when measured against English standards reveals that the American is paid more for being idle than the English worker for doing a full job. The standards of an inadequate welfare state in America are higher than the most complete and ideal socialism could provide in any industrialized country of Western Europe, not to speak of the underdeveloped lands. And when we turn to such a country as China, for example, it is apparent that the most "complete socialism" at its present economic and technological level will achieve immediately only a faster rate of capital accumulation, the immediate fruits for the population being largely spiritual—plus harder and more prolonged labour. In material terms of the broadest distribution of the fruits of modern industry among the people, to give them a more abundant life, there is today more socialism in America than in all the rest of the world combined—in fact, without straining the point too much, in terms of the abundant life for the masses there is as yet no socialism outside of America. Everywhere else socialism remains an aspiration and programme for the future.

All these self-evident facts, however, cannot hide the truth that it is the *future*, whether conceived as one or ten centuries, that outweighs the present in terms of history. If America does not learn, and learn quickly, to mobilize her potentialities more efficiently and put them to work, the future may very well belong to China in another hundred years. In the long run, as America showed during the last century, it is the rate of economic growth now that determines which shall be the leading nation of the world.

© EARL BROWDER 1960

COMMUNISM IN INDIA

By Guy Wint

I

THE EARLY HISTORY of Indian Communism took place not in India, but outside. It was the contest of small groups of Indian Marxists, in Moscow and Berlin especially, to obtain the patronage of Moscow, in order to become the properly ordained leaders of a revolutionary movement which they believed that India was ready to produce.

In India itself the Communist Party was founded in 1925. True, there had been individual Communists in India before that, but their activities were not very capable or dangerous to the government. Nor did they become any more so after the founding of the party. The intelligence system of the Indian Government at that time was unusually good, and nearly all the actions of the conspirators were known.

For this ineffectiveness, one of the reasons was the peculiar nature of the leadership of Communist Parties in Asia. India was no different in this respect from other Asian countries. The defects have been analysed very suggestively by Mr Lucien Pye in his book *Guerilla Communism in Malaya*. Most of the Communist Parties in Asia were founded by men who were by no means men of action—men who turned towards Communism as a possible way out from the evils of a collapsing society but whose desire for salvation exceeded their skill as politicians. The Asians who were the first to be fascinated by Marxist doctrine were intellectuals, often at the universities, either as professors or students. Their approach was intellectual. They wanted to be precise about the new doctrine, to dissect and grasp it. Though they may not have understood their own mental processes, most of them seem to have had an underlying supposition that the thorough grasping of the ideas was enough in itself. They were both impressed and misled by the fact that in Russia the ideas of Communism had overthrown the Tsarist empire; they assumed, in a vague way, that if correct Communist ideas were

105

disseminated, the ideas would have a life of their own, and that the walls of capitalism and imperialism would fall without the Asian Communists having done much more than propagate the doctrine. They confused the struggle for intellectual illumination with the struggle for political power. They were unaware that the essence of Communism, as understood by Lenin, is the gaining of power by whatever means offer themselves at a particular moment. Even if they were willing to take to active conspiracy, they were obsessed with the idea that power must be sought by orthodox means which had to be found out from the Marxist scriptures. That true Communist conspiracy is an obsession with power, a lightning understanding of how to get it at a given moment, and a willingness to twist all theory to justify the action which a cool consideration of events dictated, was quite beyond their understanding.

In India the early efforts of Communism were directed to trying to bring about a replica of the 1917 revolution in Russia. The Communist Party in India was to attempt a seizure of power by violence. And it was to base itself exclusively on the proletariat. The bourgeoisie were always enemies.

The October revolution in Russia had of course been brought about in this way by a conspiratorial party, which made use of certain exceptional circumstances in order to seize power at the capital. Though in theory the Russian Communist Party was a workers' party, in fact it was a group of full-time professional revolutionaries who used the worker proletariat as its tool. It had no confidence in the peasantry except as a tool for its political action, because it believed that the peasantry was an innately conservative force.

Unfortunately for the Communists, the example and inspiration of the 1917 revolution in Russia could be of little use to a Communist Party in India in 1925. True, the Indian party was confronted by an imperial government, a little like the government of Nicholas II. But there was this vital difference. India in the 20's had not been shaken by war. The government was strong, and it was remarkably efficient in defending itself against sedition.

The effective opposition to the Indian government was of course not Communism, but the nationalist movement of Gandhi and Congress. The Communist Party might have been expected to see this. It might have been expected to draw the conclusion that the best hope of furthering the revolution was to associate itself with the nationalist praty, to try to overthrow the existing government, and, in the confusion which resulted, to seize power for Communism. But at this stage all the instincts of the Communists blinded them to this evident truth. Their instincts were to recoil from anything associated with the bourgeoisie, and the Indian National Congress was essentially bourgeois. The Indian bourgeoisie at that stage was regarded as the supreme enemy—worse even than the British imperialists.

This relation of Communism to nationalism, which was to last for a very long while, is the clue to the whole history of Communism in India. In most other countries of Asia the rise of nationalism has coincided with the advent of Communism; it seemed natural for the two to go side by side because nationalism did not have a long previous history. In India it was different, Congress had been founded thirty years before the Russian revolution. It was entrenched. It did not need Communist aid. During the interval both Congress and India as a whole had been thoroughly permeated with liberal ideas. Congress and the national movement thus appeared as antagonists of Communism. They could not be simply permeated and taken over.

Because of this clash between nationalism and Communism, because Communism was not accepted by nationalism and did not know how to permeate nationalism, the Communist leaders in the early years in India were without any plan of effective action.

A picture of the despondency and futility of these years is given in a little book by an Englishman, Philip Spratt, called *Blowing Up India*. Spratt, on leaving Cambridge soon after the first world war, had become a Communist, and was sent to India as a courier and agent. He describes the rather amateur attempts to gain control of trade unions, and to agitate.

"When I arrived in India", he said, "some of the Communists understood doctrine as well as I did, but there was no activity. Clemens Dutt had given me a cipher and code and an invisible ink. All proved in vain. The code was fairly obvious and the CID men seem to have solved it at a glance. The cipher must have cost them a lot of work, but they broke it eventually. The invisible ink, alas, did not remain invisible. We used them mainly to communicate names, secret addresses, and messages about money."

Spratt describes the contact of Communism with the outside world. The difficulty for Russia was the visa policy of the Indian Governments Between the October revolution and the war, Delhi granted no visa. to Russians. Partly because of this, the direction of the Indian

Communist Party was left to the British Communist Party. But clandestine visitors did occasionally arrive from Moscow.

"At the end of 1927 we had a visit from a member of the Russian party. He was a Caucasian or Turk, to judge from his appearance. He habitually wore the red Turkish cap and passed as a Moslem. He was a good conspirator, so good that I made the romantic guess that he might be a GPU man. The police seem to have obtained no information about him, though he spent months in India and met quite a number of people. I had a long discussion with him at the top of one of the minars of the Taj Mahal. He was business-like but quite friendly."

Some of the contacts with Moscow were disturbing, even at this stage.

"The Sixth World Congress took place in the summer of 1928. Without telling the rest of us, Shaukat Usmani decided to attend it, taking three others with him. The first I heard of the adventure was a cable from London asking whether Usmani represented the party. I replied no, which of course was true. Usmani spoke at the Congress and returned to India about the end of the year. But the other three were detained in Russia. Later on an Indian from Moscow came to Meerut and had an interview with Usmani. Shortly afterwards Usmani began to behave queerly, in fact underwent what would be called a nervous breakdown. He left the party. The stranger had informed him that his three companions had been shot as spies in Moscow. Usmani had written a book about his travels through Afghanistan and Turkestan. He had asked me to write a foreword for it, which I did. When he left the party, some of the comrades turned on me and declared that I ought not to have written the foreword to his book. 'You ought to have known he was a rascal,' they said."

Spratt goes on:

"There were many strikes in 1928, and members of the party contrived to gain the leadership of some of them. We also tried in a number of instances to bring about strikes. I travelled along the East India Railway, in company with various union men, appealing to groups of workers to strike. Many of the railwaymen we brought out lost their jobs. It occurred to me sometimes that it was a little incongruous for us members of the educated class to urge these ignorant people to face such risks for a purpose which they could not understand. However, Lenin has told us precisely that was the job of the educated professional revolutionary." [1]

The Communist Party's first real success came in 1928 when it caused big and wasteful strikes in the Bombay cotton mills. The government was alerted and in March 1928 arrested thirty-one of the Communist and trade union leaders. Philip Spratt was among them. There followed the protracted Meerut trial of the prisoners which has become famous as the spectacle of a prosecution exaggerating enormously the importance of a very small conspiracy. The sentences finally given to most of the prisoners were much reduced upon appeal. The conditions in prison—the forced juxtaposition of the prisoners and their leisure for dispute—led to great divisions on Communist doctrine, and Spratt describes how various conflicting groups came into existence.

That was the end of the first period of Communism in India. The leadership was broken. The effort had been ineffectual. Communism was not a great public movement, like Congress nationalism. It went underground. And it had achieved nothing. As long as the Communists in Asia took the October revolution in Russia as their model, their results were negative.

II

There followed a period of new growth. A new group of potential leaders was recruited, chiefly in Britain. These were to become the ruling cliques of the present time: thus, as Mr Masani points out in his history of the Indian Communist Party, the Party was to be in the hands chiefly of men whose families had been rich enough to send them to Britain to study. This "upper crust" nature of the Indian Communist Party has continued down to the present. It has been important because it has given the party a curious respectability in Indian society, even though its doctrines were proposing to disrupt the society.

Another result was that throughout its history the Indian Communist Party has remained far more factional than Communist Parties elsewhere. This may reflect a national characteristic: Indians are given to faction. In India the factions claim the right to think for themselves, and to interpret for themselves the directives received from Moscow. Often they interpret them differently, and even a reasonably clear directive was not enough to put an end to the Party disputes.

[1] From *Blowing Up India*, by Philip Spratt.

At first these new groups continued to be more interested in theoretical speculation than in action. The early thirties were the culmination of the national struggle by the Congress Party against the British Raj. The most striking fact about the Indian Communists during this time was that they continued to dissociate themselves from Congress and from nationalism. Their prevailing theory was still that nationalism was a movement exclusively of the bourgeoisie, and of the Indian capitalist system. Thus a Communist Party had to regard nationalism as its enemy. The Communists could not have been more explicit about this. A Platform of Action, prepared at this time, has the following paragraphs:

"The greatest threat to the victory of the Indian revolution is the fact that great masses of our people still harbour illusions about the National Congress, and have not realised that it represents a class organisation of the capitalists working against the fundamental interests of the toiling masses of our country."

And again,

"The policy of Gandhism, on which the programme of the Congress is founded, uses a cloak of vague talk about love, meekness, modest and hard-working existence, lightening the burden on the peasantry, national unity, etc. But under this cloak it preaches and defends the interests of the Indian capitalists."

Of course, some Communists, being also Indians as well as Communist theorists, did not hide their affection for the national movement. But most of them showed themselves its opponents. This became very widely known. The Indian Communist Party was for many years regarded as anti-national. Particularly it committed the sin of opposing Gandhi. Gandhi was their most deadly opponent. He—or their public denigration of him—was the main cause of the Communist Party's slow development.

True, between 1936 and 1941 the Communist Party made a rather half-hearted attempt to modify this attitude. This was the period of Popular Front—the rally of all possible allies for Russia. Under pressure from the British Communist Party, the question was raised, Why not bring in the Indian National Congress? This was the germ of all that has followed. The Indian Communist Party began to take more interest in the national cause.

They tried to do so by filtering into Congress with the idea of capturing it, especially into its Congress Socialist wing. (At that time the Socialists did not exist as a separate party.) One of the most energetic Communists in the movement was Mr Namboodiripad, who recently has been Communist prime minister of Kerala. But it was an ineffective movement. The anti-Communist leaders in Congress were vigilant, and exposed the tactics. A number of Communist documents, showing tactics of secrecy and deception, fell into their hands and were published.

When Russia came into the war, the Communists and Congress were once again pushed wide apart. Congress opposed the war; the Communists had to mobilise every possible support for Russia. This took the rather strange form of backing the British imperialist government in India. The Communists were its willing agents, though naturally they tried to turn the co-operation to their advantage rather than to the advantage of the government. In this they were not very successful. The Home Department of the Government of India used them skilfully in mobilising pro-war sentiment among various sections of the community, especially students, and gave away very little in return. Some cells of the Communist Party seem to have actually helped the police in rounding-up Congress activists after the Congress Rebellion of August 1942. As a result the Communists disgraced themselves further in the eyes of nationalists. More than ever, the Communist Party was an anti-national party.

That was the outstanding circumstance when war came to an end, and when the struggle between the Raj and Congress was brought to a stop.

III

What follows took place against a transformed background. Two events after 1947 were decisive. One was the attainment by India first of complete self-government, and then of sovereign independence. The anti-imperialist struggle no longer existed. The other was that from 1949 onwards, China was a Communist state. And the Chinese Communist Party, though it did not willingly admit it explicitly, had seized power by its own unorthodox means, and without paying attention to Russian direction. The Chinese Communist Party was victorious not by a *coup d'état* in the cities made by a small resolute party, but by organising large peasant armies which stormed the cities and ousted the Kuomintang. Moreover it had not hesitated to co-operate with certain sections of the bourgeoisie. Communist China was thereafter a very strong state, and by its influence and example it affected the further development of Communism in India.

The independence of India opened up entirely new prospects to the Indian Communist Party. It had to write off most of its previous history as a story of failure. The most it had really achieved was to organise the nucleus of a disciplined party. That was, of course, one great asset. It was the indispensable condition for Communist revolution. But the Communist Party had not come anywhere within sight of the seizure of power. It had not tried to raise guerrilla armies, as Mao had done in China. Propaganda to students, peasants and armed forces—the penetration of trade unions—these had brought little gain. But the situation seemed likely to change.

The Communists might argue that in the past they had been unable to make progress, because there was no revolutionary situation. After 1947—the year of India's independence—the situation seemed better. Was there not now a revolutionary situation? The war had brought great social transformations. It had been a forcing house, accelerating social and political change. There had been the Bengal famine, and, after independence, partition and the ghastly communal killing. Economic suffering and political confusion—these were conditions apparently ideal for Communist strategy.

Presiding over this very uncertain situation there was, in place of the old and tried imperial government, a nationalist government which might claim to fulfil the national will, but was untested and problematical. Here too was a promising situation for Communism.

The problem for the Communist Party in India was how to turn this situation to account. Two decisions had to be made—one the attitude towards nationalism, the other the attitude towards parliamentary and democratic institutions.

The Indian Party began with the handicap of its unfortunate record on nationalism. It was obvious that it could make no real progress until it had lived this down, and had shown itself to be as vehemently nationalist as the Congress Party. Communism had to steal the leadership of the nationalist movement from Congress. This, from 1947 onwards, was in the background of the mind of most Communist leaders.

This consideration governed a great deal of the controversy which has taken place in the Indian party from 1947 down to the present day. There has been an oscillation between two radically different theories.

One is that Communism is the party of the proletariat. It must oppose all other classes. This has been the rigid or hard or left school. The other view—the rightist view—has been that it is permissible to make an alliance with bourgeois parties, or to appeal to the bourgeoisie for the furtherance of the rather vaguely conceived goal of Communism. Communism is a party in quest for power, and as its tool may use any class whatsoever. The task was to define the enemy. Allies were anyone who would collaborate against the enemy. If the enemy was defined as American or British imperialism, Indian nationalism might be an ally. It is a natural corollary that if you are following a policy of looking for allies, you avoid violence as much as you can.

Sometimes these two views have been synthesised. The Communist Party claims to be a party of the nation, and not simply of the proletariat: as such it can appeal to the middle class and to patriotic capitalists. But it must refuse to ally itself with a bourgeois party; instead—on this view—it should try to win the bourgeoisie away from the bourgeois parties. But it wants their support only, not their partnership; the driving force in such an alliance must be the Communist Party. Much of this theory was of course borrowed from China.

The second problem—the attitude towards parliamentary institutions—was harder to decide. Should Communism use violent methods for seizing power—in imitation of Russia—or should it drop these, and instead exploit the parliamentary institutions and try to come to power by their means? Should it accept the idea of peaceful change?

True, there was a clear party ruling against this second course—the ruling of the Comintern Congress of 1920 at Turin. That had regarded parliaments as a snare. It warned that Communists got elected to parliament as good revolutionaries, then became gradually interested in their parliamentary duties, and ended in believing in the infinite durability of the existing order.

To boycott parliament or to try to destroy it was the orthodox Communist doctrine. And yet in India the parliamentary institutions were there, invitingly before them. In some areas, seats were to be won almost for the asking. The Comintern theses at least allowed Communists to enter parliaments for the purpose of agitation. In South India, Communists could not make their conspiracies as if they were blind to the democratic, or quasi-democratic, political life all around them. The debates on these questions were very bitter. The Indian Communist Party was much divided by faction. At times this paralysed its actions.

The decisions by the Communist Party in India about how to act in these complex circumstances were of course influenced by Moscow. But Moscow's direction was not entirely cut and dried; the extent to which Communist action is centrally directed has often been exaggerated. Some of the national Communist parties have evidently a good deal of autonomy. But the guiding lines in the post-war years were almost certainly laid down by Russia.

In determining this strategy—whether it was to be violent insurrection or political action within the parliamentary frame, and whether or not there was to be collaboration with the national bourgeoisie—the Russian leaders, at least until the death of Stalin, were obsessed, and as it was to turn out frustrated, by their own doctrinaire interpretation of contemporary Asia. They were convinced that the Western withdrawal from Asia was a sham. Whatever the political changes which were apparently happening in the colonial territories, the Russians believed that there was no genuine ending of imperialism or of Western rule. If Britain was giving up direct power it was because it hoped to enjoy as much power as in the past, though by indirect means. For this purpose, said the Russians, Britain was transferring its authority to bourgeois governments, responsible to bourgeois parliaments, and it was confident that it would be able to bind these governments to itself, and that they would effectively prevent any victory of Communism by democratic processes. With great cunning, Britain was splitting the popular forces. What Britain was doing successfully, France and Holland might be expected to do eventually in Indo-China and in Indonesia, even though at first they were reluctant to go so far in surrendering direct rule, and tried instead to maintain their direct authority.

This interpretation was given especially clearly at the end of 1947 by Y. Zhukov, one of the principal theorists about Soviet policy in Asia.

"In those cases where the colonies are granted sham independence, it is as if the imperialists are falling back on previously prepared positions, on their second line of defence, which consists in resorting to methods of indirect rule, more often in using the whole rich store of tricks accumulated by the bourgeoisie to deceive the masses, to keep them in obedience not just by bayonets, but also by some reforms." [2]

Because it interpreted the Asian situation in this way, Russia in 1948 promoted an armed insurrection in all the colonial territories in South

[2] From *Bolshevik*, 15 Dec., 1947, No. 23.

Asia. In India this rebellion took two forms. The first was in the great cities, especially Calcutta, where the Communists organised strikes and violence. This was an attempt to copy the Petrograd insurrection of 1917. It was a dismal failure. How could Communism advance itself by disturbing the peace of Calcutta? Even if it had succeeded in organising riots on a grandiose scale, the Government of India would simply have declared a state of emergency, and moved in troops from outside to crush its conspiracy.

The second form of the rebellion was more interesting. This was an attempt to emulate the Chinese tactics, and to base the revolution not on the towns but on the countryside. There had already been a precedent for this. In 1946, in the district of Vayalar in what was then the state of Travancore, Communist propaganda had persuaded the Ezheva caste to seize an island, defy the local authorities, and set up a rudimentary administration.[3] To put down the rising, the Travancore State government had to use its army.

In 1948 the area chosen for action was Telingana. This was selected because it was on the borders of Hyderabad state and Madras, and a border region favours insurrection because the police are under different authorities on different sides of the border; this was the so-called "border doctrine" learned from the practice of Communism in China. In Telingana the Communists could rely on the bitterness of the Andhra people whose demand for a separate state had still at that time not been met.

For a time the Telingana rising appeared serious. The government machinery of civil administration could hardly operate. It seemed that here was the nucleus of something like the Chinese Red Army base in Yenan. If Communism had taken control of a larger area, the Congress government which had succeeded the British Raj might have been shaken; and the Indian Government, in its self-confidence today, may do well to look back from time to time on the dangers with which it was confronted in 1948, and to keep in mind that they may recur. But in 1948 the Indian rising could not succeed, even if it had had a leader of genius like Mao Tse-tung. The reason was that the conditions which Mao had said were necessary did not then exist in India. The base—Telingana—was too small. It was insecure. And the national government was too strong, too well organised, and enjoyed too much prestige, since it was accepted as being more truly "national" than the

[3] The Ezhevas had had a large number of soldiers in the army. They were discontented after their demobilisation.

Communists. It was easy for it to bring great force upon the rebellion from outside; and the ordinary administration was presently restored.[4]

Thus the Indian Communist rebellion failed. It came to an end when the faction in the party which favoured "activism" lost face because of the failures, and the initiative passed to the party which favoured agitation within parliament. As the Indian Communists became accustomed to parliamentary life, they became increasingly immersed in this; thus they have behaved exactly as was foreseen—with alarm—by the drafters of the theses of the Comintern Congress at Turin.

When the failure of the insurrection in India became plain, a grand inquest began in the Communist Party about its causes. The defeat suffered was in such glaring contrast with the successes in China. It was asked whether Mao Tse-tung and the Chinese Communists had the secret of a method, or a plan different from that of Communists elsewhere. Should the "Chinese Way" be adopted? With the prestige which came from their own victory, the Chinese, joining in the debate, had begun to speak more authoritatively in their statements about their own achievement. Their theorist, Liu Shao chi, had made uncompromising claims.

> "The road taken by the Chinese people in defeating imperialism and in founding the Chinese People's Republic is the road that should be taken by the people's democracy—this road is the road of Mao Tse-tung. It can also be the basic road for liberation of peoples of other colonial and semi-colonial countries, where similar conditions exist." [5]

In June 1950, just before the start of the Korean war, Peking went even further. It said that the lessons of the Chinese revolution applied to many colonial and semi-colonial countries outside Asia. It referred especially to the Middle East, Africa and Latin America.

These claims by the Chinese were naturally not very welcome to the Communist leaders elsewhere, especially as they came at a time when their efforts were meeting with humiliating unsuccess. They were challenged by the Communist Party of India. Between the party in China and the party in India there had been for a long time little contact and

---

[4] The administration had broken down because of the chaos brought about by the refusal of the Hyderabad government to federate, and by the Indian action to compel it to do so.

[5] Lui Shao-chi. Opening address to Trade Union Conference of Asian and Australasian countries. Nov. 25, 1949.

some evident rivalry. Indian Communists had been accustomed previously to expect guidance not from any Asian source, but from Communists in Britain, and it was through this channel that they had received by relay the advice of Moscow. The Indians, in their turn, had aspired to advise some of the parties of South-east Asia. They were very sensitive about being eclipsed by the Chinese.

In the immediate post-war period Mr Zhukov, laying down the official Russian view, had said that the hope of the Communist world in Asia lay jointly in China and India. But by the time of the Calcutta Youth Congress, China was in the ascendant. The Chinese had been crowned by success, and the Indians could hardly object. When, however, the Chinese began to lecture the rest of Asia upon theory, the Indians took their stand. They pointed out publicly—which no other Communists had done—that, whatever the triumph which the Chinese had won, their theory—the very theory which had won them their victory—was extremely heterodox. It was the opposite of Marxism and Leninism. Mr Ranadive, a rather mercurial person, who had seized the leadership of the Indian party by accusing his predecessor of being too tame, turned upon Mao some of the combativeness which he had formerly used upon the Indian Government and upon opposing factions in the Indian Party.

"We must state emphatically that the Indian Communist party has accepted Marx, Engels, Lenin and Stalin as the authoritative sources of Marxism. It has not discovered new sources of Marxism beyond these. Nor for the matter of that is there any Communist party which declares adherence to the so-called theory of New Democracy alleged to be propounded by Mao, and declares it to be a new addition to Marxism. It must be admitted that some of Mao's formulations are such that no Communist party can accept them; they are in contradiction to the world understanding of the Communist parties. Those who contrast the Chinese and Russian way have many things wrong in their minds. First, their idea about the Russian revolution is wrong. They think that the Russian revolution was achieved suddenly on November 7—a one-day show, a sort of coup—and forget the dogged fight for three decades, the persistent effort to win over the majority of the people during the revolution and before. They also forget the civil war. Secondly, when they contrast and uphold what they call the Chinese way they seek to reject the hegemony of the proletariat in the democratic revolution and feel that the Chinese revolution shows that the hegemony of the proletariat is not necessary." [6]

This article, in the Bombay journal *Communist*, appeared in June 1949. For the next few months sharp exchanges took place between the Indian and Chinese parties. They became a scandal among the Communists. Finally, international communism intervened, and in January 1950, the Cominform—the successor to the Comintern—publicly instructed the Indian party to conform to the Chinese view.

The Indians held out for another six months; then capitulated. They confessed that they had slandered Mao. They recanted and admitted that Mao was a true Leninist and Stalinist, and that their own opposed views had been a "full-fledged Trotskyite thesis". They asked that their previous views should be entirely cancelled and no longer regarded as authoritative.

Yet that was not the end. A year later, Moscow itself had second thoughts about Chinese claims. After all, if China was to lay down the law for all Communist Asia, and if its revolution was to be accepted as the standard Asian pattern, the Russian Government might well fear for the future of its prestige in the Asian continent, and for its own share of the leadership in promoting revolution. A discreet reduction of China's claims was to be expected. It came in the form of a statement by a group of Soviet orientalists who in November 1951 met in Moscow and defined the Russian view. "The experience of the Chinese revolution", they said, "is of immense significance. But it would be risky to regard the Chinese revolution as some kind of stereotype for people's democratic revolutions in other parts of Asia." [7]

IV

The failure of violence brought about a time of extreme confusion in the Indian Communist Party. It was a time of factionalism, intrigue, recrimination. The British Communist Party lent a hand in trying to restore unity. In the end, in September 1951, Ranadive was replaced. A new programme was begun. It was rather vague, but it looked again towards mobilising other classes besides the proletariat, and perhaps to collaborating temporarily with other parties.

[6] Editorial. *Communist*, Bombay, Vol. 2, No. 4, 1949.
[7] *Izvestiya Akademii Nauk. Seruja Istorii i Filosofii*, Vol. 9, No. 1, 1952.

The Communist Party made some solid gains at the general election at the end of 1952. It became the second largest party in the central parliament—though with 23 members a very long way behind Congress, which had 362. It made sensational advances in Madras and Hyderabad. Its electoral strategy was good. It concentrated its effort, and in the states won more seats than the Socialists, though it gained only half as many total votes as the Socialists. In the whole country it polled 4 45% of the total votes.

Its propaganda began to become increasingly effective. The Communists had begun to achieve successes in "boring from within". Their targets were students, Gandhians, youth, scientists, the civil service, the army, the professions. Their cultural organisations were by now impressive. Directing this side of their work was a section of the party known as the Technical Organisation. It was extremely secret, the details of its activities being unknown to most of the senior officers of the party. It is surmised that through such underground action the Communists have made secret converts of some individuals in high places. At critical moments they may act in the interests of the party rather than of their government.

The Party even attempted to build up a following among business men, on the ground that Communism would promote their interests against those of American and British capitalism more effectively than the bourgeois parties could be expected to do.

The Party intensified its efforts at capturing the trade unions; here it had to face an able trade union leadership dominated by Congress. But little by little it has gained, and Congress has given ground.

Very strangely, the Communists neglected the peasants, though here the ground might have seemed fertile, and though there was the example of China's peasant revolution to encourage them.

The Communists found a particularly promising line in championing the regional particularism in India. When the British left India, the boundaries of provinces were very arbitrary, and were made more so by the integration of the Indian states which followed independence. The sub-nations of India—Marathas, Telegus, Gujaratis, etc.—feel their national identity strongly, and there was agitation that they should be grouped into their own separate provinces. For a time the central government opposed, because it feared that "national provinces" might defy the centre. The Communists opted completely for the regrouping, and began to profit accordingly. But this grievance which played into their hands was removed in great part by the recommendation of the

States Reorganisation Commission, which were implemented in 1957. Only the Marathas in Bombay continued to be denied what they conceived to be their rights. Thus, among the Marathas, Communism increased. But in the end the Marathas also achieved their demand.

The next crucial date in the history is 1956—the visit of Krushchev and Bulganin to India. At this time, Russia's main aim was, not to promote Communist revolution in all countries, but to thwart America, and to use Communism in all lands as an instrument in Russia's plans for safeguarding and defending Russia as the homeland of Communism. The Indian Communist Party, no less than Communist Parties elsewhere, was to be used.

Clearly it seemed to Krushchev that one of the most valuable allies of Russia against the West would be the nationalism of free Asia. He set himself to woo Nehru, stressing that Russia was the champion both of neutralism and anti-colonialism. Its aspect as aspostle of Communism was allowed to fall into the background. It seems plain that the Communist Party of India was told to join in. Nehru, in Communist eyes, became a "progressive". Criticism of him was dropped.

V

If Communism had had to fulfil for a long while the role of a minor ally of Congress, it would have been an unglorious end for a party which had been ambitious to become all powerful. But events came to its aid. A new phase began, almost by chance in the early part of 1957 when there took place the second general election in India. The Communists contested it. Though they experienced some reverses in districts where they had been strong, they won very nearly a clear majority in Kerala—which was made up of the former princely states of Travancore and Cochin and the former Malabar district of Madras. Because of the confusion and disunion among Congress, Socialists and Independents, the Communists were, under the constitution, the best entitled to form a government. This they did.

Thus in Kerala the Indian Communist Party had achieved its Yenan. It gained a foothold on power. It became a government instead of opposition: it was the first Communist government in the Commonwealth. But it was a peculiar Yenan. The Communists in Kerala had come to power by constitutional means, and their hands were tied by the constitution because they were a state government and not a national government. The state government had limited rights. Its ports were controlled by the federal government. The central government made it plain that as long as the Communist government acted constitutionally, it would be tolerated. The moment it exceeded its powers under the constitution, the federal government would step in, as it was constitutionally entitled to do, and supersede the Communist government.

In such limiting circumstances, the Communist government in Kerala could hardly light the torch of national revolution. At their most optimistic, they calculated that their achievement in Kerala would become known elsewhere—that it would swing the vote at the next general election in the Communist favour in at least two provinces, Bengal and Andhra. A little later other states might vote Communist. In the end the Communists might come to prevail at the centre. And when they did so, they would no longer be fettered by the constitution. The real Communist revolution could begin.

These were the considerations which led the Communists to take office. Doing so was a repudiation of the resolutions of the Comintern Congress at Turin in 1920 which had never been rescinded, and which laid it down that parliamentary action was a snare for Communist parties; if they became entangled in parliaments they would lose the zest for revolution. The Indian Party was willing to take the risk, presumably with the sanction of Russia.

The Communist government in Kerala lasted for two years, and caused changes both in the Indian Communist Party as a whole, and in Communist Parties elsewhere in Asia. Communists combine great attention to orthodoxy in debate with complete opportunism in practice. For a time it looked as if a new way for Communists to come to power was disclosing itself in the countries of Asia which had genuinely democratic systems of government. If the ballot box had created a Communist ministry in Kerala, it could do so over wider areas. A section of the Burmese Communist Party suggested that the Burmese party should abandon its civil war, emerge from the jungle, surrender, become constitutional and win at the hustings what it had failed to win from its ambushes.

In the Indian Party itself, the moral was drawn that a peaceful and constitutional way to victory might at least be a possibility; and the party constitution was reformed in order to facilitate it. At a Party Congress at Amritsar in April 1958, the party organisation was converted to look less conspiratorial and more like an ordinary democratic party: the aim was to attract the voter, and not to scare him. Party cells were replaced by party branches.

The difficulty about the new policy lay in the fact that, for it to be successful, the Kerala government had to achieve such success that it would attract the admiration of the electorate in other Indian states and in other Asian countries. This it failed to do—partly because its powers were so limited. Communism could not make sweeping changes in the social structure. And, as a Communist government, the ministry could not even rule competently over the existing society and economy. New capital, which was needed to galvanise the economy, was afraid to come to Kerala.

Instead, the Kerala government, all of whose actions were scrutinised by nearly all the newspapers of India, became increasingly notorious for malpractices. It interfered with the machinery of justice; it connived at the party setting up private courts in villages, to terrify its opponents; it was involved in financial scandals, in which profits from state transactions were siphoned off to Communist Party funds. Rather surprisingly, the government antagonised the university students. Throughout nearly all India, student opinion had begun to move against Communism.

The major legislation by the Communist government was a land reform, and a reform of the schools administration; and this last brought about its downfall. In fact the schools bill, which caused so much commotion, was on much the same lines as legislation in some other states of India. Kerala has a very large number of schools, started by churches but paid for by the state. The school managers receive the money from the government, and pay the teachers, and they have been in the habit of deducting from the teachers' salaries a percentage for the school expenses. The bill stopped this by providing that the salaries should be paid by the state directly to teachers. Also it required the school managers to limit their appointments of teachers to candidates on a roster approved by the government. Allegedly this was a means to obtain Communist control of the schools. But it was not a very extreme means.

The schools bill stirred up the implacable hostility of the Catholic Church, and this communicated itself throughout the state. Congress, both in Kerala and in India as a whole, became more aware of the danger of allowing Communism to become consolidated in one state of the Indian Union. In June 1959 the opposition parties launched a campaign of direct resistance to the government, based on the techniques of Mr Gandhi.

At first the campaign miscarried. The Indian intelligentsia regarded the tactics with distaste. To subvert a parliamentary government not through parliament but by mass agitation was against the spirit of the constitution. But the campaign, once launched, showed how great and genuine was the popular dislike of Communism. If the campaign had continued, it would probably have ended in bloodshed on a large scale. In June, Nehru paid a visit to Kerala, and suggested to the government that the proper way to deal with the situation was to hold new elections. This it refused to do.

"It appears", said Mr Nehru at the time, "that a very considerable upsurge among the large masses of the people is taking place in Kerala against the government there. I cannot measure the extent of this, but there can be no doubt that it is on a big scale. I do not think that any particular legislative measure, even though it is disliked, could have led to this upsurge. It is rather due to a feeling of distrust against the government that has grown in the course of the past few months."

The agitation grew. Nehru's daughter, who was President of Congress, joined with the forces at Delhi which were pressing for the suppression of the Kerala government. Nehru, after much hesitation, gave way before them, and in August the ministry was deposed and replaced by Presidential rule, that is, civil service rule. That is the procedure laid down by the constitution in case of the breakdown of proper government in a state.

In a subsequent debate in parliament, Mr Nehru said that he had been induced to act, not because the federal government objected to legislation by the Kerala government, but because of the "sense of unease" in the state. "Things were happening there which were progressively lessening the freedom of speech and action of the people. The idea was spreading that no protection could be given by government authorities and police to those opposed to them."

VI

1959 was a bad year for the Indian Communists. Hardly had they taken stock of the blow in Kerala, than they were put by China's border policy in exactly the situation which it was important for them that they should avoid. China, aware of its growing strength, anxious to wreak revenge on India for harbouring the Dalai Lama, incensed by the habit of Mr Krushchev of treating China and India on equal terms, and perhaps also feeling that India's friendship was no longer an asset to it, began to lay claims to borders which it had formerly enjoyed in the days of the Manchu Empire. This led to a claim for about 40,000 square miles of India's North East Frontier Agency, and a large portion of Ladakh. Chinese troops began to filter in to the contested areas. There were clashes with the Indian border police. Peking and Delhi exchanged stiff notes. Indian feeling was deeply stirred.

The Indian Communist Party could not avoid declaring its attitude. The crisis raised again the issue which throughout its history has been the bane of Indian Communism—its relations with nationalism.

The Party saw rising once again the spectre which had haunted it from its beginning. Was the Party to align itself with the demands of the Chinese Communist Government, and to become regarded again in India as an anti-national party as during the war years? To do this threatened its prospects in the new elections which had been fixed in Kerala as the way of ending Presidential rule. Or should it support Indian rights, and perhaps be condemned as heretical or revisionist by other Communist Parties of Asia? The Indian Communists have been much less lucky than the Chinese. In China, because the Kuomintang proved an incompetent defender of national interests against Japan and the West, the Chinese Communists were able to step into its place, and claimed convincingly to be the better champions of nationalism. The Chinese Communist Party made its policies at home; they were not dictated by Moscow, and in fact they often were contrary to what Moscow had recommended. By contrast, the Indian Communist Party, in large matters, had been controlled persistently by Communists from outside. That was the fact which Congress and Jawaharlal Nehru used against them with deadly effect. One of the mistakes of the West is to suppose that Nehru takes a soft line about Indian Communists. On the contrary, he has hammered them consistently and with skill. Always his accusation has been that their hearts are not in India, but in Russia or China.

The Indian Party was, as usual, divided about what it should do. Its Bengal members, living nearest to the threatened area, were, rather strangely, among those who wished to back the Chinese case. Ajoy Ghosh, the Secretary-General, went to Moscow, and from there to

Peking in order to try to make Chou En-lai more aware of the Party's embarrassment, and to beg him to be more circumspect. His visit was in vain. A meeting of the Party's Central Committee at Meerut, after hearing Ajoy Ghosh's report, managed to agree on a resolution which pledged the Party to support India in its case on at least a part of the disputed frontier, but with reservations, and with a demand for negotiations with China.

The resolution did not save the Communist Party from defeat in the Karala election. But the severity of its defeat can be exaggerated. The Party increased its vote: the opposition, now united, increased still more.

VII

Some of the party leaders may have been encouraged to stand up to China by advice from Moscow. China and Russia are engaged in a subtle covert struggle for the patronage of Communist Parties in Asia. Moscow may have welcomed China's roughness towards India as a way of attracting back interest from Peking to itself. Anxious for its own reasons to set limits to China's expansion in Asia, it may have deterred the Indian Party from making China's path smooth, just as in its public pronouncements it showed itself lukewarm about China's claims.

The Indian Party has always paid closer attention to Moscow than to Peking. Moscow's influence had been responsible in part for the oscillation in the attitude towards the bourgeoisie. Ultimately the changes were traceable to Russia's foreign policy. At periods when Russia found itself reasonably secure at home, it was able to devote itself wholeheartedly to propagating the Revolution. At such times, Communist Parties everywhere were exhorted to take the hard line of attacking the whole society. But at times when the Russian home-land was threatened internationally, Russia's interest was to gain allies. It was wooing other governments, and did not wish them to react too sharply because of the activities of their domestic Communists. So at such times, Communist Parties would be instructed to drop their intransigence, and to try to make common cause with the "progressive" elements among the bourgeoisie. At these phases, Communists in India would try to work with Congress; in 1941 they worked even with the British, against Congress.[8]

[8] In India before independence the situation was even more subtle. Russia had *three* aims: to bring about revolution, to embarrass the British Government in

Since independence in India, the Communists have shown a fairly frequent disposition to woo the lesser bourgeoisie for a common front against capitalism. How far this is an Indian idea, how far it is Moscow-inspired, is not altogether clear.

Moscow lays down the general principles of Communist policy. But usually it prefers to leave the local Communist Parties to apply them. The communication between Moscow and national parties is often conducted in broad daylight, in the form of pronouncements by Soviet leaders or articles in the Soviet press. Local Communists are alert for their appearance. But in India the Party has always been divided into quarrelling factions, and not every faction was willing to accept the Moscow Line.

A curious point may be noted. In the Indian Communist Party, no man of genius has yet appeared, either as theorist or man of action. There has been nobody like Mao Tse-tung who has worked out a new strategy in the teeth of orthodoxy, not even a competent theorist like Liu Shao-chi; though there has been plenty of pamphleteering. India has contributed almost nothing to Marxist thinking or Marxist action.

What are the long-range prospects of Communism in India? It is impossible to prophesy anything about India while Nehru lives or remains supreme. Today is Nehru's India. With him gone, there will be rapid change. But whether a revolutionary situation will develop, it is not possible to say.

Psychologically, Communism will continue to have a powerful attraction in India. This has been especially well stated in the latest book on the subject, *Communism in India*, by Gene Overstreet and Marshall Windmiller. The authors say:

"The possession of a cohesive world view endows the Party worker in India with an unusual degree of militant zeal. Gandhi himself has recorded his admiration for the ability, energy and dedication of the Indian Communists. In addition the ideology has a potential attraction for a large segment of the Indian population—a body of alienated intellectuals who are contemptuous of the traditional scheme of rulers and who bitterly distrust the Western liberal system. The Party itself, as a social institution, offers a new sense of personal identification to those who have renounced old bonds."

India (except for the brief period in the war against Hitler), and to win over Indian nationalism. Policy was according to the priority it gave to these various ends.

In the long run, it may be the psychology which counts. If democratic India can offer rival attractions, the Indian Communist Party will remain in the wilderness. If the Indian Communist Party seems to offer paternal authority to a distracted nation, its prospects will be brighter.

© GUY WINT 1960

INTERNATIONAL COMMUNISM:
THE PRESENT PHASE

By Wolfgang Leonhard

SINCE STALIN'S DEATH the World Communist Movement has entered a new stage. The Soviet leaders' visit to Belgrade (May 1955), the recognition of "varying paths" to socialism, and the 20th Party Congress (February 1956), with its strictures on Stalin and Khrushchev's secret speech, appeared for a time to be endangering Moscow's hitherto unquestioned role of leader of the World Communist Movement. The spring and summer of 1956 brought evidence of centrifugal tendencies and of contradictions within the World Movement. Oppositional thoughts and demands and even theoretical concepts hitherto only whispered in intimate conversation, now came into the open. But, since the late summer of 1956, the swing has been in the opposite direction. Aspirations of autonomy have been progressively curbed, and attempts towards reform have been checked. Moscow has succeeded, step by step, in re-establishing its grip on the Communist World Movement; and further moves along this line may well be expected.

In the following pages an attempt is made to set out the main features of what has been happening with regard to the European Parties.

Belgrade and the Varying Path to Communism

Under Stalin Moscow's absolute control over the World Movement rested not only on Soviet power, on party discipline, and on the machinery for the control of members and officials of the various parties, but also on four politico-ideological principles which provided the "basic justification". These were:

(i) The leading role belongs to the Communist Party of the Soviet Union (which implies the subordination of the other parties).

(ii) All Communist parties must follow the "example of the Soviet Union" (which precludes alternative paths to Socialism).

(iii) In 1948 the Yugoslav Communists, having broken with Moscow, had passed over into the "imperialist camp" (and must, therefore, be implacably opposed).

(iv) The infallibility of Stalin. (This, though never explicitly proclaimed, had become a matter of course for any Communist Party members.)

These four principles were incumbent on all Communists except the Yugoslavs. Accordingly a departure from them by the Moscow leadership must entail considerable repercussions in the World Movement.

But this is just what happened after Stalin's death—particularly in 1955 and 1956.

As early as the summer of 1953 less and less reference was made in the USSR to the writings of Stalin. Some were withdrawn from circulation. Certain Stalinist dogmas were attacked albeit—up to February 1956—without mention of Stalin's name. Soon after Stalin's death the anti-Yugoslav campaign was modified. The slogan "Struggle against the Fascist clique of Tito and Rankevich" was dropped.[1] Attacks on Yugoslavia became rarer. From August 1954 Yugoslav Communists once again were referred to "positively".[2] On May 14th, 1955, the hitherto outlawed Yugoslavia was mentioned in *Pravda* as a socialist country. On arrival at the Belgrade airport, Khrushchev explained that Moscow's whole anti-Yugoslav campaign was the work of "Beriya, Abakumov and others": the anti-Yugoslav allegations had been "fabricated by enemies of the people who had treacherously infiltrated themselves into our ranks".[3] For our present purpose the fact that this assertion was untrue is irrelevant; what is important is that a tenet of Stalinist dogma had been dropped.

The rapprochement with Yugoslavia necessitated the dropping of a further Stalinist tenet—that whereby all countries must follow the "example of the Soviet Union". And this was done, openly, in the Belgrade Declaration of June 2nd, 1955, in which the Soviet leaders approved the Yugoslav conception that "differences in the concrete forms of Socialism are exclusively the concern of the individual countries".[4]

---

[1] May 1st, 1953, was the first occasion when the Central Committee's slogans included no anti-Yugoslav slogan. (*Pravda*, 22nd April 1953.)

[2] *Pravda*, 29th Nov. 1954.

[3] *Pravda*, 27th May 1955.

[4] *Isvestiya*, 3rd June 1955; and *Pravda*, 3rd June 1955; also the Belgrade *Borba*, 3rd June, 1955.

The question of the "varying paths to Socialism" seemed so important to the Moscow leadership that it received considerable prominence at the 20th Party Congress (February 14th–25th, 1956). Apart from Khrushchev himself, the right of every country to find its own way to socialism in accordance with its own conditions, was explicitly affirmed by Suslov, Shepilov, Molotov, Kaganovich and Kuusinen. Even the possibility of attaining socialism by parliamentary means seemed now to be under consideration by the Soviet leadership. Their aim was to facilitate a rapprochement with Yugoslavia and with the social democratic parties of western Europe.

The results, however, were not those expected by Moscow. In spite of the cautious formulation of its wording the approval of varying paths to socialism gave ideological justification to those within the World Communist Movement who were working for reform. Its impact was all the greater because at this same 20th Party Congress the cult of personalities was officially condemned, other Stalinist theses modified, Yugoslavia the subject of favourable mention, and the message of greeting from the hitherto outlawed Marshal Tito received with rousing applause. Khrushchev's secret speech at the private session of February 25th, served even more strongly to emphasise the importance of the change of line.

Although the Party leadership had strictly defined the scope and limits of the departure from Stalinism, the new line of the 20th Congress was a matter of extreme importance for the World Movement. The new ideological pronouncements and practical measures all showed a withdrawal from Stalinism. It was inevitable that an impression should arise in Communist circles throughout Europe, that the proceedings of the 20th Congress marked the beginning of a serious re-examination of the negative aspects of Stalinism. Many further harboured hopes of a new development of World Communism on autonomous and independent lines.

Dissolution of the Cominform

The criticism of Stalin and the pronouncement on varying paths raised the question as to whether the Information Bureau of the Communist and Workers Parties (Cominform) could or should continue to exist. It is true than in late December 1955, Khrushchev had declare himself in favour of its continued existence at a session of the Supreme Soviet—a sign that it had become a subject of discussion within the Soviet leadership. The 20th Party Congress avoided the issue. The

Stalinist instrument for the control of the Eastern Bloc and the Communist World Movement, was not mentioned—but there was also no suggestion of its imminent dissolution, although this would be a natural implication of the new line.

The appeal for the liquidation of the Cominform came not only from the Yugoslav Communists, but apparently from other quarters as well. It is perhaps significant that the first news of its approaching end came not from Moscow, but from a Radio Zagreb report (March 22nd) of a conference in Rome.

The official communiqué of its dissolution (April 17th, 1956) was most cautiously worded. By mid-April it is probable that Moscow was aware of the dangerous results that might follow from the admission of past mistakes. It was, therefore, explicitly declared that the Cominform had played "a positive role", and that it had been "an important factor for the strengthening of proletarian internationalism". Its positive features were said to include the strengthening of ties and the mutual exchange of experience, but also "the strengthening of the influence of the Communist parties among the masses", although in fact in almost every Communist Party outside the eastern satellites, both membership and influence had appreciably declined since 1947.

As with the dissolution of the Comintern in 1943, it was now explained that in view of the altered circumstances the Cominform had fulfilled its purpose. Therefore, it was decided to bring to an end the activities of the Information Bureau and the publication of its weekly paper *For a Lasting Peace, for a People's Democracy*. Again, as in 1943, the hope was expressed that the Communist parties would find new and fruitful forms for the establishment of close relationships.[5]

In subsequent editorial comment, mention was made of the increasing independence of the various parties. *Pravda* laid down "that it was demanded more than ever of the individual parties that they pay careful attention to the characteristics and special conditions of their countries". It was, therefore, for these parties to develop a policy "that would be most suitable to the special characteristics and circumstances of the peoples in question",[6] other Communist organs uttered similar sentiments.[7]

The Yugoslav Communists welcomed the abolition of an organ

[5] Communiqué in *For a lasting Peace for a People's Democracy*, Bucarest, 17th April 1957; *Pravda*, 18th April 1956.

[6] *Pravda*, 18th April 1956.

[7] *Neues Deutschland*, 20th April 1956.

which they had had every justification to hate, but protested against the wording of the official communiqué. The Cominform had in no way played a positive role or contributed to the strengthening of internationalism; it had in fact done internationalism considerable harm. The Yugoslav theoretician, M. Pijade, declared that "a future serious historical analysis of this organisation would show that it played no constructive role".

But apart from the Yugoslav Communists, the Italian party leader, Palmiro Togliatti, went far beyond the terms of the official communiqué. He spoke of "certain negative aspects" of the Cominform; it had been an error, in 1948 and 1949, to have "interfered from outside in the affairs of the Yugoslav party". There had been no regular discussions in the Cominform, and the activity of the Information Bureau had proved "increasingly unproductive". Of great significance was the hope expressed by Togliatti that there would from now on be "a greater easing" and "a greater tendency to adapt the activities of the Communist parties to the conditions of each particular country".[8]

Two Tendencies within the Movement

It thus became apparent in the spring of 1956 that the proclamation of the new line and the dissolution of the Cominform had not led, as the Soviet leadership had hoped, to a rapprochement with the West European Social Democrats (in April 1956 the Socialist International had rejected all advances[9]); on the other hand there was a quickening of the urge towards autonomy within the Communist movement.

This process developed rapidly from April to June 1956. Within the USSR and the Eastern Bloc there were a series of de-Stalinisation measures—criticism of Stalin, open admission of error and injustice, the revision of the writing of history, the campaign for socialist legality, the rehabilitation of former "enemies of the people", the publication of Lenin's will. These were not without their effect on the Communist parties outside the Eastern Bloc.

There came increasing evidence of the existence of two differing trends. On the one side were the Stalinist forces who had accepted, albeit reluctantly, the new Party line as developed at and after the 20th Congress, but who were now concerned with doing all that was possible to minimise the importance of the change, and to put limits to its practical implementation. On the other side were the reformers who

[8] *L'Unita*, 18th April 1956.
[9] *Socialist International Information*, London, 14th April 1956.

not only welcomed the recent developments, but regarded them as a hopeful beginning of a fundamental departure from Stalinism.

Signs of these two trends came to light in a number of the parties. In East Germany the Party Secretary of the Erfurt district had to protest against the "hostile" rumour, of conversations taking place with the fraternal parties in Moscow, about a split within the Communist Party of the Soviet Union into a Stalinist Communist Party and a National Communist Party.[10] It is certain that this version of the rumour was exaggerated, but there is other evidence of the two trends. The Hungarian publicist, Tibor Tardos, declared at a meeting of the Petöfi Circle in August 1956: "There are at present two tendencies within our party—one, the dogmatic Stalinist tendency, the other determined to give effect to the resolutions of the 20th Congress." [11] Marshal Tito declared in his speech in Pola on November 11th that the question now was "whether in the various Communist parties the new spirit would prevail, the spirit which had originated in Yugoslavia, and which had been apparent in the 20th Congress . . . or whether victory would go to the Stalinists".[12]

The reformers were encouraged by two events in June 1956. From June 2nd to 22nd Marshal Tito, once the main target of Cominform attacks, was in the Soviet Union on an official invitation. At the end of his visit a joint declaration was made by the Soviet and Yugoslav parties which went far beyond the Belgrade declaration and the 20th Congress. This declaration stated "that the paths of socialist development in the different countries and in different circumstances are diverse", and again "richness (or variety) in the forms of the development of socialism is a factor for strength": thus the example of the Soviet Union is no longer obligatory in either the *path towards* or the final attainment of Socialism. As to the relations between the two Communist parties, it was laid down "that neither side has any desire to force upon the other its own conception of the ways and means of socialist development". Co-operation should take place "on a basis of absolute freedom and absolute equality, of friendly criticism and comradely exchange of opinion".[13]

Although this agreement was merely a Soviet-Yugoslav affair, it

[10] *Das Volk*, Weimar, 26th July 1956.
[11] Quoted from *Ostspiegel*, SPD-Pressedienst, Bonn, No. 34, 24th Aug. 1956.
[12] *Borba*, 16th Nov. 1956.
[13] *Information Bulletin of the Socialist League of Yugoslav Workers*, Belgrade, Nov. 1956; also *Borba*, 21st June 1956.

necessarily encouraged hopes in other Communist parties that they too would be freed from their subordination to Moscow, and would obtain new forms of co-operation just as Tito had done.

Tito's visit to the USSR coincided with a spate of discussion in the various parties over Khrushchev's secret speech. It is true that some of the main points of the speech had been made known to party leaders of the various parties as early as March,[14] but the publication of the whole text at the instance of the American State Department on June 4th, gave party members a far fuller picture than could have been obtained from the hints in the party press. Discussions on Stalin therefore, acquired a new intensity. Both problems, Stalin and the autonomy of the non-Russian parties, were thus inextricably joined.

Togliatti's "Polycentric System"

Discussions reached such a pitch that the leaders found it no longer possible to maintain silence. The first to speak was Togliatti. On his return from Belgrade (where he had been conferring with the Yugoslav leaders in late May) came his now well-known interview in the *Nuovi Argumenti*.[15] In this he went further than any previous official pronouncements as regards both Stalin and the greater independence of individual parties.

The importance of Togliatti's remarks is that (contrary to what had appeared in the Soviet Union) his criticism was not limited to Stalin personally, but directed at the whole system. The attitude of the 20th Congress regarding Stalin's errors was "not satisfactory". The Soviet leaders would continue to be affected by the cult of personalities so long as they regarded Stalin's personal failings as the cause of all evil. The real problem was why and how Soviet society "could have, and had, strayed from the true path to the point of degeneration". Quite apart from Stalin's shortcomings there was the "excessive and increasing hold of the bureaucratic Party machine on the economic and political life of the Soviet Union". It would not be wrong to say "that it was in the party that began the harmful restrictions on democracy and the gradual usurpation of power by bureaucratic organisations".

After a detailed analysis of "the risk of bureaucratic degeneration" Togliatti demanded a greater independence for the individual Com-

[14] *Neues Deutschland*, 4th and 18th March 1956; *Szabad Nep*, 15th March 1956; *Trybuna Ludu*, 10th March 1956; *Rudé Pràvo*, 7th March 1956.
[15] *Nuovi Argumenti*, No. 20, 16th June 1956; also *Unita*, 17th June 1956.

munist parties. The criticism of Stalin had "called forth a demand for progressively greater autonomy". This could be "only beneficial to our movement". The position had altered to such an extent that the Soviet example "must no longer be obligatory". The Communists in every country should take as starting point their national traditions and conditions. There was being evolved a "polycentric system" and even within the Communist World Movement it was no longer possible to speak of a single leadership.

Togliatti's ideas in themselves were not new. Similar ideas (some even more uncompromising) had been held by oppositional Communists in the 20's and 30's, and, since 1948, by the Yugoslavs.[16] What was new and important, however, was the official leader of a Communist party going far beyond official Soviet pronouncements, but not breaking with Moscow.

The Party leaderships in other countries were obviously uncertain as to how far Togliatti's speech should be taken as "official". This explains why extracts of the speech were published in the Polish, Hungarian and in some East German newspapers, and were praised in the Party organs of the West European parties.[17] Togliatti himself, on June 24th, returned to the charge and proposed that Communist parties be given full freedom to enter into bilateral relationships so as to attain complete understanding and mutual confidence.[18]

By the end of June 1956, things had gone so far that for the first time since the Yugoslav break, a number of party leaderships openly criticised Moscow. The French, British and American parties declared, as Togliatti had done, that Soviet statements regarding Stalin's errors had been unsatisfactory; what was urgently necessary was a thorough investigation into the causes of the Stalinist dictatorship. The American party went on to criticise Khrushchev for his silence regarding the anti-semitic excesses of the Stalin era, and coupled this criticism with the demand for equality of rights for all parties.[19]

Moscow's Counter-measures

These critical declarations by party leaders coincided with the strike in Posen which began on 28th June and soon became a rising. Moscow

[16] See Kardelj and Velko Vlahovic in the *Bulletin*, Belgrade, Aug. 1955.
[17] *Friheten* and *Drapeau Rouge*, 19th June 1956.
[18] *Unita*, 26th June 1956.
[19] *Humanité*, 19th June 1956; *Daily Worker*, London, 22nd June 1956; *Daily Worker*, New York, 24th June 1956.

seemed threatened with loss of control of the process of de-Stalinisation. It was then, on June 30th, that the Central Committee in Moscow adopted the resolution "The cult of personality and its results", published in the Soviet press on July 2nd, and subsequently in all Communist papers throughout the world.

The aim of this resolution was to restrict criticism of Stalin, to halt the campaign for de-Stalinisation, and to oppose the "too far-reaching" efforts towards autonomy within the Communist World Movement. According to the new definition, the cult of Stalin's personality had not "affected the nature of the socialist state." The idea that Stalin's dictatorship was a result of changes in the social order of the USSR was sharply rebutted. Of prime importance to the non-Russian parties was that the thesis of varying paths was now severely restricted. From now on it was the "specific features" of the various paths to socialism that were discussed. Communists, "in the circumstances of the moment" (a noteworthy limitation), would take heed of the special characteristics of their country. The dissolution of the Cominform should not lead to the conclusion that "international solidarity and the need for contact between revolutionary Marxist-Leninist fraternal parties had lost their importance". "Ideological unity" and "the spirit of proletarian internationalism" were particularly emphasised in the resolution.

This declaration by the Soviet leadership on July 30th, 1956, marks an important turning point. Criticism of Stalin and affirmation of the varying paths into socialism were progressively toned down. Moscow's concern once more to centralise the World Movement became progressively clearer. A few days later (July 26th) *Pravda* laid down in a leading article that development towards socialism was a single, world historical process; and had nothing to do with the "fantasies of certain theoreticians", "who wished to reach socialism along their own path and not along the same path as the others".

"Unity cast in a single mould" was just as necessary as the "relentless opposition to any appearances of revisionism". This line was even more strongly emphasised in a leading article of *Kommunist*.[20]

Moscow's Bilateral Conversations

It is important to note that Moscow's change of line took place in late June and early July 1956 and not, as is often assumed, after the Hungarian revolution of October. On the 26th July Moscow had signed the Soviet-Yugoslav party declaration. But on the 30th June the turning

[20] See also *Kommunist*, No. 11, 1956.

point was marked by the resolution on "the cult of personality and its results", and during July and August the change of tone was progressively more clearly emphasised, particularly so in the confidential circular to the leaderships of the east European parties dated August 21st, containing the warning against the Yugoslav example.

However, the re-establishment of Moscow's control of the World Movement could only be effected by indirect means. In the summer and autumn of 1956, so soon after the pronouncement on varying paths, the criticism of Stalin and the dissolution of the Cominform, it was not possible for the Soviet leadership *openly* to commit itself to the creation of a new international world centre. This had to take place indirectly, by means of bilateral conversations between the Soviet leadership and the leaderships of the other parties. Between early July 1956 and the end of the year the following bilateral conversations took place in the Kremlin:

Date	Party	Soviet leaders present
7th July	Belgian	Khrushchev, Pospelov, Ponomarev
10th July	British	,, ,, ,,
11th July	Italian	,, ,, ,,
29th Aug.	Canadian	,, ,, ,,
5th Sept.	Luxemburg	Suslov, Ponomarev
10th Sept.	West German	,, ,,
29th Sept.	Norwegian	,, ,,
9th Oct.	Swiss	Pospelov, Ponomarev
11th Oct.	Austrian	,, Suslov
12th Nov.	Dutch	,, Ponomarev, Kuusinen
28th Dec.	Israel	Suslov[21]

Suslov's "common features and laws of development"

These bilateral conversations were obviously Moscow's first step in the attempt to resume control of the World Movement.

October in Poland and the Hungarian revolution in October–November, led to an abrupt sharpening of effort. The Soviet leadership was obviously intent on withdrawing the concessions of 1955–6 and on tightening up the screws, even at the risk of appreciable loss of membership, mass resignations and a decline in political prestige.

The first decisive declaration along these lines was made by Suslov on the 39th anniversary of the October revolution.[22] Far more attention was given to international Communism in this speech than had

[21] Soviet Press, *passim*.   [22] *Pravda*, 7th Nov. 1956.

hitherto been customary. Suslov made no mention of the dissolution of the Comintern but stressed the "unshakeable loyalty" of the Communist parties to the principles of international Communism. He also formulated four "common features and laws of development" which, apparently, were essential for the victory of Communism and the establishment of a socialist society. First came "the establishment of the political power of the workers with their progressive element at their head", i.e. the supremacy of the Communist Party in the form it had taken in the Soviet Union; and the "determined defence of the achievements of the socialist revolution against the attacks of the former exploiting class", a formula intended ideologically to justify both the use of force in the country concerned as also armed intervention (as in Hungary). Although Suslov allowed there to be certain differences "arising out of the practical circumstances of the country in question", the formulation of common laws of development obviously meant that the Communist parties of the Eastern Bloc must act solely on the lines of "the Soviet example".

In spite of the bilateral conversations and Suslov's common "laws of development" there were still appreciable difficulties to be overcome. Soviet intervention in Hungary had given the western Communist parties a severe shock. In France and Italy there had been mass resignations. Even old party functionaries of long standing had left the party in protest. Again in the smaller parties like the British, Swiss, Dutch and Danish, the leaderships had to contend with serious difficulties. Many members and party officials of standing with the public at large, turned their backs on the party. In a number of countries diffident groups were formed with their own periodicals and their own organisations. Even in the parties of the Eastern Bloc there were serious differences of opinion. In the SED in East Germany, Wolfgang Harichs' platform, representing a reformist tendency, was given wide publicity. But a few weeks later Harichs and his closest collaborators were arrested.[23]

Apparently unmoved by all this Moscow redoubled its efforts to revive the defunct Cominform, or at least to bring into being a new organisation on the same lines.

The campaign began with a declaration by the SED *Neues Deutschland* of November 28th to the effect that the attacks of reactionaries "made

[23] See *Western Communist Parties' Reaction to Events in Hungary* and *Aftermath of Hungary among Communists in the West*, Evaluation and Research Section, Radio Free Europe, Munich, 6th Dec. 1956 and 26th March 1957.

it desirable to find new forms of co-operation and consultation". It was essential to promote the unity of the World Movement and all parties must find "a clear answer" to this problem. On the same day the Austrian *Volksstimme* declared itself in favour of the creation of an international organ for Communist parties, and announced that the Austrian Party had "undertaken steps in this direction but there were still differences of opinion in certain parties". The Moscow *Mezhdunarodnaya Zhizn* (No. 11 of 1956) also demanded new forms of association for the various national parties. It was necessary to strengthen ideological unity and "regularly to exchange experience". The Communist World Movement is a single ideological movement; its power lies in its common ideology and in "the unity of its strategic aim"; paths to socialism should not stray in different directions but should be all along the same route.

By the end of 1956 strong resistance to the new attempts to centralise became apparent, and not only in the rank and file of the parties but also in certain leaderships. Apart from the Yugoslavs, Polish and Italian leaders opposed these attempts. From December 19th to 29th, 1956, conversations took place at Belgrade between the Polish and Yugoslav parties, and concluded with an official announcement that "bilateral relationships between the parties are the proper form, under present conditions, for co-operation between Communist and Worker Parties". In this declaration it was explicitly declared that the various countries make their way into socialism along different paths and thereby enrich socialist development.[24] In December 1956 the 8th congress of the Italian party recommended that "each Communist party should decide its own path of progress and struggle for socialism". In consequence "it is important to preserve autonomy in examining and assessing the possibilities of applying Marxist-Leninist principles in given national conditions". The Italian resolution came out explicitly in favour of bilateral relationships within the World Movement. These relationships demand "mutual respect and friendly criticism" but must avoid "interference in the internal affairs of other countries". Of particular interest was a declaration rejecting the return to a centralised organisation of relationships between parties. If problems of special importance were to arise, international meetings might well take place, but "not to formulate binding resolutions binding on all but merely to clarify attitudes".[25]

This resolution of the Italian party was the last declaration of this kind.

[24] *Information Bulletin*, Belgrade, Jan. 1957.
[25] *Unita*, 15th Dec. 1956.

From early 1957 Moscow's pressure became stronger. In the first week of January a meeting took place in Budapest between Khrushchev and Malenkov, and Zhivkov (Bulgaria), Kadar (Hungary), Georgiu Dej (Rumania), and Novotny (Czechoslovakia).[26] Subsequently the party leaderships in Germany, Czechoslovakia and France declared for a renewed centralisation of the World Movement under the leadership of Moscow. After a visit to Prague the French party leader, Raymond Guyot, declared that the dissolution of the Cominform "could at no time lead to the lessening of the international obligations. On the contrary it could only mean a strengthening . . . We are determined ever more fully to develop our mutual relationships and consultations".[27] On April 15th, 1957, the East Berlin radio declared that it was now only a question of time before the search for new methods and forms of co-operation between parties would result in an appropriate conclusion. In mid-June the Czech leader, Hendrychs, spoke in favour of common negotiations between a large number of parties, and suggested the foundation of an international newspaper[28] for theoretical matters. At the beginning of July the Rumanians declared for an international newspaper.[29] After this preparation, Boris Ponomarev (in charge of the Soviet Central Committee's section for the International Movement) laid down in the September issue of *Kommunist* (No. 12—1957) that a "further consolidation of international co-operation" was the most important pre-condition for the "success of the Communist movement as a whole, and for that of each individual party in particular".[30] Ponomarev specifically referred to the wishes expressed by other parties, and asked for "periodical large-scale international conferences of Communist and Worker Parties".

At that period the Soviet leadership was still hoping to win over the Yugoslavs. Moscow's anti-Yugoslav campaign, which had flared up again after the Hungarian revolution, began to die down in the spring of 1957, and for a time ceased. In mid-July 1957, there was a meeting in Moscow of Soviet and foreign party leaders attended also by the Yugoslavs, Kardelj and Rankovich.[31] In early August, Khrushchev and Tito met in Rumania. Following this meeting came a communiqué stating that both sides "attached special importance to the strengthening of the

[26] *Pravda*, 6th Jan. 1957.
[27] *Humanité*, 16th Feb. 1957, and Gunther Nollau, *Die Internationale* (Cologne, 1959), p. 230.
[28] *Rudé Pràvo*, 19th June 1957. [29] *Scinteia*, 9th July 1957.
[30] *Kommunist*, No. 12, 1957. [31] *Pravda*, 19th July 1957.

unity and brotherly co-operation of Communist and Worker Parties".[32] This formula did not mean (as Khrushchev later maintained) the recognition of a central Moscow leadership of the World Movement, but could perfectly well be reconciled with the idea of co-operation of equals which Belgrade had long maintained.

Moscow failed to win over the Yugoslavs. Between August and November 1957 it became clear to the Yugoslavs that the toning down of the anti-Yugoslav campaign was merely a tactical step on the part of Moscow, aimed at discrediting Yugoslavia with the West and the neutral states of Asia and Africa; and so bring her back to incorporation in the Eastern Bloc.

The International Communist Congress

After these preparations there took place in Moscow (November 14th–19th) the largest international congress since the Comintern Congress of the summer of 1935. The aim was quite obviously to reassert the unity of the World Movement under the leadership of Moscow. The congress came after the festivities to mark the 40th anniversary of the revolution and the successful launching of the two sputniks.

The congress was in two stages. From November 12th to 14th only the twelve ruling parties in the Eastern Bloc took part. On the 16th to 19th there was a (far less important) conference of representatives of sixty-four parties. It is worth noting that certain parties were not invited to this international congress, including the American, South African, Philippine, Irish, Egyptian, Burmese and Iranian parties.

It was officially announced by the Russians that the total membership of Communist parties throughout the world was then "over 33 million" as against 4·2 million in 1939 and "over 20 million" in 1945.[33] Most were in the ruling parties of the eastern states. First came China (13 million), followed by the Soviet Union (7·2 million), Czechoslovakia (1·4 million), Poland (1·4 million), East Germany (1·2 million) and North Korea (1·165 million). In the other Eastern Bloc states party membership was under a million—Rumania (600 thousand), Bulgaria (484 thousand), North Vietnam (460 thousand), Hungary (383 thousand), Albania (48 thousand) and Outer Mongolia (38 thousand).[34]

[32] Boris Ponomarev's speech on the 75th birthday of G. Dimitrov, Radio Moscow, 18th June 1957.

[34] *Yezhegodnik Bolshoi Sovietskoi Enfsyklopedii*, and *Politicheskii Slovar* (Moscow, 1958).

The November conference produced two documents that laid down the new line—the politically more important "Declaration of the Representatives of the Communist and Workers' Parties of the Socialist Countries", and a "Peace Manifesto" signed by all the sixty-four parties present.[35]

It appears from the official reports that the congress did not take place without friction.[36] There were obviously differences of opinion as to reference, in the Declaration, to the leading role of the Soviet Union, and also as to what form future co-operation should take. The Soviet Union (represented by Michael Suslov) secured Mao Tse-tung's support of the leading role of the Soviet party. Mao, who spoke first, declared that the World Movement, just as every small party group, must have "a head". The Chinese party was not worthy of this position. It was true that China had considerable experience in the construction of socialism, but the Soviet experience went back for more than forty years. Also Chinese industry was still small, and China did not possess even a quarter of a sputnik whereas the Soviet Union had two sputniks. Soviet reports give a number of the leaders as stressing the leading role of the Soviet party including Ho Chi Minh (North Vietnam), Enver Hodzha (Albania), Hendrych (Czechoslovakia). Zhivkov (Bulgaria), Dashin Damba (Mongolia), Chivu Stoica (Rumania), Kim Ir-sen (North Korea) and Walter Ulbricht (Eastern Germany). There being no mention, in this connection, of Gomulka (Poland) and Kadar (Hungary) it may be assumed that these two leaders spoke in a contrary sense. The final declaration was a compromise, no mention being made of the leading role of the *Communist Party*, but only of the Soviet Union (*as state*) within the Eastern Bloc.

Another cause of disagreement was the form of future international co-operation. It appears from Polish reports that Suslov had urged periodic global conferences, on the lines of the former world conferences of the Comintern. This was opposed by the Poles under Gomulka on the grounds that past experience of centralised organisation, both in the Comintern and the Cominform, had been unsatisfactory. He (Gomulka) would agree to the proposal only on condition that global conferences were not allowed to interfere in the internal affairs of the various parties, and that resolutions must be passed by all parties *unanimously*. Also, the only participants at global conferences should be leaders elected by the parties—by which provision Gomulka

[35] *Pravda*, 22nd and 23rd Nov. 1957.
[36] *Trybuna Ludu*, 29th Nov. 1957; *Neues Deutschland*, 30th Nov. 1959.

was obviously aiming to avoid the risk of Moscow dismissing unamenable party leaders, and putting in their place Moscow stooges as the "real representatives" of the party in question. In the official Declaration Suslov's demand for world conferences was toned down. It stated that: in addition to bilateral conversations "more comprehensive conferences of the Communist and Worker parties could be instituted".

The Declaration demanded the consolidation of the unity of the socialist camp and ordered Communists to defend their historical, political and social achievements against all ranks of their enemies, they were to consolidate the Warsaw Pact, and wage a determined battle for the destruction of survivals of bourgeois nationalism and chauvinism.

The thesis of varying paths to socialism was even further watered down. It is true that the Declaration mentioned the "manifold nature of national characteristics and traditions", and the necessity to pay attention to the concrete historical circumstances of each country; but it went on to say that the cause of socialism would be harmed if one were to "exaggerate the role of these differences, or use them as an excuse to stray from the universally valid truths of Marxism-Leninism regarding social revolution and the building of socialism". Thereby it was made clear than any future attempts of any Eastern Bloc state to find a path to socialism other than that of the Soviet Union, would be regarded as harmful to socialism.

The Declaration contained eight "laws of development, universally valid" for all socialist countries binding them to the Soviet example. The most important are:

(i) "The leadership of the toiling masses through the working class whose core is the Marxist-Leninist party, in the carrying out of the proletarian revolution in this or that form, and in the establishment of the dictatorship of the proletariat in this or that form."

(ii) "The defence of the achievements of socialism against the attacks of external and internal enemies."

Thereby ideological sanction was laid down for the harnessing of all Eastern Bloc states to the Soviet example, and also for any armed intervention (as in Hungary).

It was further made incumbent upon Communist parties to fight against "Dogmatism" and "Revisionism". "Dogmatism" substitutes quotations and pedantry for examination of the actual facts, and it leads to the weakening of ties between the party and the masses. "Revisionism" is taken to include all reforming trends which lead to opposition to "the historical necessity of the proletarian revolution and the dictatorship of the proletariat", to the "leading role of the party", to "the principles of proletarian internationalism" (i.e. subordination under the USSR), and to the "Leninist principles of party organisation" (i.e. the dictatorship of the leaders over the members). "Dogmatism" was only condemned; on the other hand "Revisionism" was declared to be, in certain circumstances, the main danger and to be a form of expression of bourgeois ideology which weakens the revolutionary energy of the working class, and which furthers the maintenance or restoration of capitalism. This apodiectic formulation was, however (apparently at Polish insistence), modified by an additional clause that in certain phases of development, "Dogmatism" could also become the main danger for certain parties. "Every Communist party must decide which danger it finds the greater in any given period."

The Declaration mentions the necessity of the co-operation of Communists with socialist parties—but specifically excluded the latters' "right wing leaders", in other words, the Communists will only co-operate with those members and officers of socialist parties who place themselves under their lead.

The "Peace Manifesto" passed by the sixty-four parties at this same conference, was on the same lines as the Declaration of the twelve parties; but is less radical in tone and more designed to suit the needs of fellow-traveller organisations such as the World Peace Movement.

At this November conference, the Communists of all countries— except Yugoslavia—received a binding general line. In spite of some concessions, Moscow had succeeded once more in concentrating the World Movement in its own hands, although perhaps not quite to the extent that had been the case under Stalin.

The Campaign against "Revisionism"

The November conference was scarcely ended when Moscow launched an open campaign against "Revisionism". On January 17th, 1958, *Pravda* drew attention to the growing tendency of certain "wavering elements" in the Communist World Movement. *Moskva* (No. 1, 1958) wrote "Revisionism as well as National Communism must be rebutted and destroyed through ideology—Either we destroy Revisionism or Revisionism will destroy us; there is no third way."

It is true that in the World Movement there were tendencies working for greater independence, for varying paths, for a radical retreat from

Stalinism, and for free and independent creative development of the theory and practice of Marxism.

Well-known old Communists in many countries gave in their resignations and founded journals, groups, organisations and parties of their own. In Italy there appeared the *Corrispondenza Socialista* edited by Eugenio Reale, also *Passata e presente* edited by Antonio Giolotto. In France reformist views found expression in Lefevre's *Voies Nouvelles*, and in *La Nouvelle Reforme, Tribune de Discussions* and *La Commune*. In Great Britain Communists who had left the party in 1956 and 1957 founded *The New Reasoner*, and in Brazil (which has the most important party in South America) a reformist wing defected in May 1957 under Agildo Barrato, and took the name of *Corrente renovadera*. Strong reformist tendencies were noticeable in the Dutch and Danish parties. The former party president, Aksel Larssen, left the Danish party with a number of followers, and founded his own organisation.[37]

In March 1958, when Moscow's anti-revisionist campaign was in full spate, the Yugoslav Communists published the draft of their party programme to be submitted to their congress in Ljublijana in April. As a reply to the Yugoslav draft, the Moscow anti-revisionist campaign was intensified. In four long-winded articles in *Pravda*, the Yugoslavs and like-minded Communists elsewhere, were sharply attacked.[38]

The Yugoslav congress was boycotted by the parties under Moscow's leadership. Only the Danes and the Norwegians sent delegates, and the Italians, Indonesians and Tunisians were represented by observers. After several days of discussion the Yugoslav congress accepted the new party programme, which has since been the main target of the ideological attacks of the Eastern Bloc and the World Movement. This is not the occasion for a detailed analysis of the Yugoslav programme or of the ensuing Soviet-Yugoslav controversy. But some of the principal points of differences are as under:[39]

(i) Instead of the stereotyped Moscow propaganda about imperialism and the "sharpening of contradictions", the Yugoslav programme recognises and analyses new phenomena such as the nationalisation of whole industries, the growth of state investments, State control over private capital, and the development of regional and international economic organisations.

[37] *Problems of Communism*, No. 4 (July/Aug.), 1958 (*The Spectre of Revisionism* by Donald S. Zagoria).
[38] *Pravda*, April 5th, 7th, 9th and 14th, also *Kommunist*, No. 6, April 1958.
[39] *Programme of the League of Yugoslav Communists*, Belgrade, 1958.

(ii) Instead of the Moscow thesis that only the Communist parties are the champions of the working class and of socialism, the Yugoslav programme declares "the view that Communist parties hold the monopoly for every form of socialism, and that socialism can only find expression in these parties, is wrong in theory and is harmful in practice". Today there are various forces working for development towards socialism—trade unions, national revolutionary movements, social democratic parties, etc. The Communist parties led by Moscow do not understand that the "circumstances of the struggle of the working class have changed", and this has led to the "isolation" of these parties.

(iii) Instead of Moscow's insistence on a single leadership, the Yugoslav programme declares that forms of co-operation of the international working class movement "cannot be thought out or laid down in advance by any centre". Accordingly it recommends relations between the parties and organisations as between equals. Collaboration must be based upon "a full equality of rights, and the scrupulous avoidance of any attempt to dictate views or to interfere in the internal affairs of other parties". Co-operation on an equal footing must not be limited to the Communists, but should embrace socialist parties of various trends and other progressive parties and movements.

(iv) Instead of the eight general rules of development of the Moscow November Declaration, the Yugoslav programme recognises the tenet of varying paths. The aims of socialism are to be implemented by the peoples of the world, "in various ways and by various means". Socialist development depends upon the conditions actually prevailing, on the class power-relationship, on the stage of economic development, on the political structure, on tradition, and on the social consciousness of the masses of each individual country.

(v) As against the Soviet economic system Yugoslav programme declares that planned economy should not mean "that the whole of society is turned into a machine, where everyone is told in detail what he has to do, so that the individual can no longer create". Economic planning must confine itself to the laying down of certain basic priorities, so that "in the framework of these the free initiative of the enterprises in market conditions" may have full play.

(vi) As against the Soviet thesis of *"partiinost"* (party-mindedness) and "socialist realism" the Yugoslav view is that a Communist party's duty does not consist in acting as "dogmatic judge" with regard to trends, schools and styles in learning and the arts. It is important to avoid letting "learning and the arts become a tool for the furtherance of current political aims".

(vii) As against the Moscow thesis of the leading role of the party in all realms of life, the Yugoslav view was that the "proclamation of the Communist party's absolute monopoly of political power as a universal and eternal principle", is a "dogma that cannot be maintained". The ruling parties should not take decisions that should more properly fall into the competence of bodies elected with the participation of all citizens: to do so would lead to "a limitation of the importance and the role of popular representation".

The publication of the Yugoslav programme was followed by a flood of anti-Yugoslav articles from all party papers in the Eastern Bloc.[40] But little attempt was made to tackle the particular problems brought up by the programme. Instead of discussion, there were merely the usual stereotyped attacks—"liquidationism", "lack of recognition of the differences between capitalism and socialism", "capitulationism" and finally "the setting aside of the great experience of the Soviet Union".

The Cominform Periodical

The struggle against "Revisionism" played an outstanding role in the *Problems of Peace and of Socialism*—the periodical of the Moscow-led Communist movement appearing from September 1958.

The decision to start a periodical had been decided at the November congress, but preparations took up several months. In March 1958[41] organisational details were settled at a meeting in Prague; in mid-May the Soviet ideologist A. Rumyantsev resigned from his post as chief editor of *Kommunist*, and shortly afterwards was appointed chief editor of the new publication in Prague. In a leading article of the first issue

---

[40] *Shen min Shi bao* (6th May), *Tvorba* (8th May), *Zeri i populit* (11th May), *Neues Deutschland* (14th May), *Rudé Pràvo* (19th May), *Tribuna Ludu* (21st May), *Rabotnitchesko Delo* (22nd May), *Scinteia* (25th May). For the Yugoslav side see *Socijalizam*, Belgrade, No. 1, 1958.

[41] *Rudé Pràvo*, 10th March 1958, and *Pravda*, 11th March 1958.

it was stated that its main task would be the propagation and further elaboration of Marxist-Leninist theory, and of the "programmatic document—the Declaration of the Congress of the Communist and Worker Parties". This meant that the November Declaration of 1957 had become the directive for the periodical's political line. The struggle against "Revisionism" was strongly emphasised. The new periodical regarded "as its foremost duty the struggle against any appearance of bourgeois ideology and especially against Revisionism—the main danger for the Communist movement at the present time".[42]

Just as with the former Cominform, the new periodical "would not be an organ that gives orders". It was to be regarded rather as "an international tribunal for the interchange of opinions and experience between fraternal parties". In view of what is known about the Comintern and the Cominform this declaration should not be taken too literally. The first number was issued in sixteen languages—Russian, Chinese, Czech, Polish, German, Rumanian, Bulgarian, Hungarian, Albanian, Korean and Viet Namese; and in English, French, Italian, Swedish and Spanish. From November 1958 a Dutch edition was also published, from January 1959 a Japanese and a Mongolian—so that in the autumn of 1959 it was appearing in nineteen languages.

Basic ideological articles of importance for all of the movement under Moscow's leadership were mainly prepared by Soviet authors. They contained frequent attacks on "Yugoslav Revisionism". Simultaneously it has become apparent that an attempt is being made to work out a common general line with regard to new problems by means of ideological, political, international conferences summoned by the editorial board. Since the summer of 1958 there have been four such conferences —"The Economic Crisis and the Working Class" (Prague, June 1958), "Theory and Practice of the so-called Human Relationships" (Rome, late 1958), "The Role of the Bourgeoisie in the National Liberation Movement" (Leipzig, May 1959), "European Integration—Contradictions of Capitalism and the Working Class" (Prague, June 1959). So far the top leaders of the various parties have not attended—the participants being second-grade ideological functionaries. It is quite possible that in the future these conferences will play a more important role, and that their political significance will increase.

The Growing Importance of International Communism

Since the November conference of 1957, a noticeably greater em-

42 *Problems of Peace and Socialism*, No. 1 (Sept. 1958).

phasis has been placed upon international Communism by the Soviet Union. This trend is still too fluid to justify firm conclusions; nevertheless there are certain points that should be noted:

(i) *Kommunist* and *Partinaya Zhizn* now publish much more in international Communism than was the case under Stalin and between 195 3and 1956.

(ii) The Soviet *Political Dictionary* (September 1958) contains far more and fuller entries on international Communism than was previously the case.

(iii) In the textbook *Istoriya SSR*, *Epokha Sotsiyalizma* and in the new textbook for party history, Soviet developments are linked more closely with the developments of the World Movement than in previous textbooks. The history of the Comintern is given in greater detail.

(iv) The series *The Library of Scientific Socialism* (started in the autumn of 1958 and due by the end of 1960 to issue seventy of the most important of political writings) contains not only the classics (Marx, Engels, Lenin), Stalin and Khrushchev, but also works of "the leading protagonists of the International Communist Movement". These include Mao Tse-tung, Lin Shao-chi, Chou En-lai, Pieck, Thorez, Duclos, Togliatti, Novotny, Ulbricht, Gheorgiu Dej, Foster and Dolores Ibarruri.

(v) At the 21st Congress (January 29th–February 5th, 1959) far more attention was given to international Communism than had been the case at the 20th Congress. At the 20th Congress fifty-five delegations had been present—at the 21st Congress seventy. At the 20th Congress the Soviet economic boss, Pervukhin, had answered the greetings of the foreign delegates in three brief sentences. At the 21st Congress, Khrushchev, in his general report, devoted great attention to the World Movement and described the Soviet Party Congress as "a magnificent demonstration of the unity, the strength, and the determination of the International Communist Movement".

The days when Stalin could refer to the Comintern as *lavochka* (junk shop) seem now past. The importance attached by the Soviet leadership to the World Movement may well increase still further in the near future.

© WOLFGANG LEONHARD 1960

AUTHORS OF PAPERS

JANE DEGRAS works at the Royal Institute of International Affairs where she has edited three volumes of *Soviet Documents on Foreign Policy, 1917–1941*, and is now working on an annotated selection of Communist International documents of which the first volume (1919–22) appeared in 1956, and the second (1923–8) will appear in 1960.

RICHARD LOWENTHAL was educated in Berlin and Heidelberg, and came to Britain in 1936. As Correspondent and Commentator for *The Observer*, he has in recent years specialized on the Soviet bloc and Communist affairs. He is the joint author with Willy Brandt of a political biography of the late Ernst Reuter, and is at present working on a comparative study of totalitarian revolutions.

ROBERT NIGEL CAREW HUNT (1890–1959) was educated at Bradfield and Merton College, Oxford. In World War I he served in the Oxford & Bucks Light Infantry, and from 1919 to 1954 he worked for the Foreign Office. From 1954 he was Lecturer and Supernumerary Fellow of St Antony's College: he also paid a number of visits to the United States where he gave lectures and took part in conferences. His best known work is *The Theory and Practice of Communism* (first published 1950, 5th revised edition 1957). Other books include *Calvin* (1933), *A Guide to Communist Jargon* (1957) and *Books on Communism* (1959).

EARL BROWDER was for many years leading member of the American Communist Party, and was member of the Executive Committee of the Comintern from 1935 to 1940. He was expelled from the Party in 1946. His latest book is *Marx and America* (1959).

GUY WINT has a long connection with India dating back to 1937 when he wrote *India and Democracy* (in collaboration with Sir George Schuster). During the war he worked in Indian External Affairs Department. Later he was a leader writer on *The Manchester Guardian*. His books include *British in Asia* and *Spotlight on Asia*.

WOLFGANG LEONHARD was educated in the USSR, and held prominent Party posts in the Soviet Zone of Germany after World War II. In 1949 he left for Yugoslavia and now lives in Western Germany. His books include *Die Revolution entlässt ihre Kinder* (1955)—English translation *Child of the Revolution* (1957); and *Kreml ohne Stalin* (1959).